THE EIGHT
COMPETENCIES OF
RELATIONSHIP
SELLING

Also by Jim Cathcart

The Acorn Principle

Inspiring Others to Win

The Professional Speaker Business System

The Sales Professional's Idea-A-Day Guide

The Winning Spirit

Speaking Secrets of the Masters

Rethinking Yourself (audio & video)

Be Your Own Sales Manager

Relationship Selling

Insights into Excellence

Selling by Objectives

Win Through Relationships (video)

Think Service (video)

Meeting with Success (audio)

Helping People Grow (audio & video)

SuperStar Selling (audio)

The Business of Selling

Relationship Strategies (audio)

Communication Dynamics

THE EIGHT
COMPETENCIES OF
RELATIONSHIP
SELLING

How to Reach the Top One Percent in Just Fifteen Extra Minutes a Day

Jim Cathcart

CEO and Founder, Cathcart Institute, Inc.

Leading Authorities  Press

Washington, D.C.

Leading Authorities Press
1220 L Street, N.W.
Washington, D.C. 20012

ISBN 0-9710078-1-0 (alk.paper)

Library of Congress Cataloging-in-Publication Data
Cathcart, Jim.
    The eight competencies of relationship selling : how to
reach the top 1% in just 15 extra minutes a day / Jim Cathcart.
      p. cm.
    Includes bibliographical references and index.
    ISBN 0-9710078-1-0
    1. Selling. 2. Relationship marketing. 3. Customer relations.
4. Sales personnel—Training of. I. Title: Relationship selling.

    II. Title.
    HF 5438.25 .C368 2002
    658.85—dc21

                                    2002072988

Printed in Canada on acid-free paper that meets
the American National Standards Institute Z39-48 Standard.

First Edition

10 9 8 7 6 5 4 3 2 1

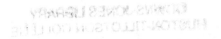

Advance Praise for
The Eight Competencies of Relationship Selling

"As a gymnast, almost every day, my goal was to
train about 15 more minutes than the rest of my
teammates. That little extra focus over a few years
led to some perfect 10's at the Olympic Games.
Perfection does take time, and Jim Cathcart
has perfected Relationship Selling. Read this book,
written by one who lives the principles he teaches,
and see what 15 minutes a day can do for you!"

PETER VIDMAR, Olympic Champion,
co-author, *Awaken the Olympian Within*

"When Jim Cathcart speaks on sales, everybody
listens! Now the man who 'wrote the book' has
written *the* book for everyone who has chosen
sales as a profession. We are living in a time when
'customers for life' is the goal of every
professional sales representative. Cathcart has
broken the code. You owe it to yourself and your
customers to catch Cathcart's formula for the
eight competencies that will start a new wave
of top performers."

FRANCIS X. MAGUIRE,
former Senior VP Federal Express

"Jim Cathcart is recognized as the world's expert
on Relationship Selling. This book only serves to
enhance and further prove that mantle.
Read this book. It is great!"

BILL BROOKS, author, *High Impact Selling*

"Jim Cathcart practiced Relationship Selling long before he penned the phrase in his book by the same name. I witnessed it firsthand many times since my first encounter with Jim back in 1979 when I hired him as a seminar speaker. The professional relationship we developed over the ensuing years was indeed built on friendship rather than manipulation —the key element of his sales philosophy. Jim exhibited that he really cared about us as a client. Over the years I hired a number of top-notch, celebrated and internationally known speakers and sales trainers for regional seminars and national conventions. Jim Cathcart was the only one that was invited back for several encore engagements. The impact of his appearances was ALWAYS measurable by the results achieved by my franchised dealer audiences. Not only did he use relationship selling to endear my entire organization to him, but Jim taught us to use the same philosophy to become the largest company of our kind in the world."

GARY GORANSON, founder, WorkEnders, Inc.

"Jim Cathcart's *The Eight Competencies of Relationship Selling* is head and shoulders above the proliferation of sales and customer management books. It imparts the comprehensive knowledge needed to achieve top 1% sales performance, deliver value throughout the customer lifecycle, and build a lifetime relationship with the customer."

ROBERT JURKOWSKI, Chief Operating Officer, Silicon Energy Corporation

"In times of rapid change, your sales experience could be your worst enemy. *The Eight Competencies of Relationship Selling* will help you break out of your sales autopilot with a renewed sense of purpose and greater profit! This book takes the best from the past that still works and adds the new proven competencies that you need to make relationship selling work for you and those you serve."

TERRY PAULSON, PH.D., author,
They Shoot Managers, Don't They?

"Relationships rule in today's environment where products and services become commodities in a heart beat. And Jim Cathcart knows more than anyone about leveraging the power of relationships to increase your sales. This book goes beyond 'why to' explanations to provide the 'how to's' you need to succeed with honor and integrity. You can't afford not to read this book— it's a sure bet that your competitors will."

RANDY PENNINGTON, author, *On My Honor, I Will*, and creator of POSITIVE PERFORMANCE®
Management

"If anyone lives what he preaches, it's Jim Cathcart! The ability to execute on his life's mission of emphasizing the importance of relationships and helping other people achieve their goals has been Jim's gift to us all."

PETER DAVIS, CEO, IDEA Health
& Fitness Association

"Whether you're a fledgling salesperson or a 30-year veteran, this book will give you powerful tools to help you make your numbers . . . in sales . . . or in life."

CHARLIE PLUMB, CAPT. USN, professional speaker, author, and former POW in Vietnam

"There's a reason why *Relationship Selling* is a sales training classic: it comes from the mind . . . and heart of America's foremost expert on sales. Jim Cathcart has the combination. He understands that there is more to a sale than an exchange of cash and product . . . successful selling, long term, is a matter of relationships and no one knows that better or says it better than Jim Cathcart. Cathcart puts the fun into selling. If you are going to read one book on selling . . . this is the one!"

T. Scott Gross, author, *Positively Outrageous Service*
and *Microbranding*

"This book is absolutely packed with results driven sales skills! Every individual responsible for sales results from the President of an organization to a first year sales person should read this book."

Scott Ulberg, President, Ulberg Group

"Jim Cathcart is one of those rare people you meet in life that isn't satisfied with just being good. Jim is committed to excellence and mastery, both in his personal and professional life. If you are interested in being great, not just good at sales, you'll want to read this book! Jim will take you to a new level of competence because he understands the heart and mind of sales. In addition to making a profit, this book is about developing yourself as a person. No one says this more beautifully than Jim."

Sheryl Marks Brown, Founder,
Institute of Fitness Psychology

"The current era demands that we develop e-contact skills as well as eye-contact skills. Jim Cathcart spans both eras. He mastered the past two decades with his original book *Relationship Selling* and now he offers us updated ways to become masters of a new era.

The Eight Competencies of Relationship Selling is a complete, random-access, digital, print and audio resource. Clearly Jim gets the point that you, the learner, should determine how you access the information."

TOM ANTION, Internet marketing expert and business communications specialist

"Jim can say more in a paragraph than most authors say in a whole chapter. Valuing your time as if it were his own, he distills his wisdom to the most precious pearls that you can put to use immediately!"

PAMELA LARSON TRUAX, co-author, *Performance Counts* and *Market Smarter Not Harder*

About the Cover

A rowing team works as one seamless unit, yet is made up of unique individuals. In order for it to be successful, this team must have the complete commitment of each of its members. They must immerse themselves in the activity of rowing and release their individual interests and concerns so that the group can work as one.

The same is true for sales competence. Many different skills are required in order to excel in sales. One must be able to manage oneself, target the right prospective customers, marshal the resources that will help make the sale, communicate clearly and convincingly, connect with all types of people and much more. But in order for a salesperson to sustain a successful sales career, all these skills must work in concert. It is not enough to merely be strong in a few areas. All eight sales competencies must be highly functional, whether through personal strength or through the intelligent use of resources.

Each person on a rowing team is necessary if the team is to remain competitive. And all must regularly exercise their skills and expand their abilities. But, when one rower doesn't stay in shape or improve with the team, all the others will feel their limitations.

Likewise you and I as sales professionals must attend to each skill-set on a regular basis. This will keep us in shape for the long run and give us the mastery needed day to day.

This book provides you with scores of ideas and brief exercises, that you can use in merely fifteen minutes each day, of focused attention on sales improvement. You can use it to keep your "team" of talents and skills at the top of their form for you and ever-ready to reach the top one percent of achievement.

To my son, Jim Cathcart, Jr.
a natural leader
and a man whom I admire.

Jim, I want to grow up to be just like you.
Dad

Contents

Contents

Foreword

I used to believe that persuasion was the key to success in selling. My personal success, in a number of direct selling efforts, was primarily due to being able to "talk people into buying." But then I discovered that people weren't giving me referrals to others, and I wasn't getting much, if any, repeat business. My sales reputation was fine in the office, but awful among my new customers. I quickly realized that my customers were not swearing by me, they were swearing *at* me.

That is when I learned that selling isn't just about getting to the top. It is also about being able to stay there—to belong at the top, especially in the eyes of your customers.

Jim Cathcart will show you how to get to and stay at the top of your field. He knows because he has done it. He has risen from obscurity to the top of his profession. As a young salesman in the 1970s he struggled to earn the trust and respect of his prospective customers. In doing so he discovered that he gained more sales as a result of the person he had become than he gained from the things he said to persuade others to buy. He also learned how to reach the top one percent of any group or organization.

You can become a top one percenter too.

And you can do it without any advanced degrees, without any big single achievements, without any powerful connections or astounding talent.

Jim learned that top one percenters think differently about what they do, build relationships in advance of needing them, take personal responsibility for making things happen, intelligently work the odds, intentionally form habits that work, know the payoffs of each of their activities, are impatient with those who don't take charge of their own lives and careers, and are generous with their time and resources toward worthy recipients. He also learned early on that by simply devoting one hour per day in study in a particular field, within five years, you can become a national expert in that field. And Jim certainly achieved that in *two* fields—professional selling and professional speaking.

Let Jim Cathcart teach you how to be one of those people who not only gets a lot of sales, but also earns the loyalty of their customers, their colleagues, and their company. Let Jim teach you how to be one of the sales professionals to whom the others look for leadership.

Let him teach you how to make your example the standard by which many in your industry pattern their own careers. Let him teach you how to win the awards and honors you want, not just through hard work, but also by systematically becoming the kind of person who deserves to win such awards and honors.

Let Jim Cathcart lead you through the eight competencies of Relationship Selling. Jim practices what he preaches. I have always admired his dedication to making himself the best he could be. As Jim's career evolved, I saw the strength of his wisdom in many areas of business.

Jim was born and raised in Little Rock, Arkansas, with few assets beyond his will to succeed. He worked at a variety of jobs until he discovered that he could succeed at anything as long as he had a good plan and consistently worked it. When I met Jim Cathcart, he was a successful professional speaker living in Broken Arrow, Oklahoma, and I was a native New Yorker working as a college professor at the University of San Diego. An unlikely duo, perhaps, but we hit it off immediately. We quickly became business partners and best friends. That was in 1979. Today, I am still impressed by Jim's success, his focus, his wisdom, and, above all, his character.

He has been inducted into the Speaker Hall of Fame by the National Speakers Association and was the recipient of the Cavett Award in 1993 and the Golden Gavel Award in 2001, placing him in the top one percent of professional speakers worldwide. He got there by sheer strength of conviction and willingness to do what was necessary to earn his success. Sure, he is bright, and yes, he has done some amazing things over the years, but Jim Cathcart's success has come about primarily from working his plan.

I have benefited greatly over the course of these last 20 plus years from my association with Jim. By reading this book, you too will realize that his wisdom works. His success sells. Enjoy reading this book and achieving an astounding level of success in the field of sales!

—Tony Alessandra, Ph.D., CSP, CPAE,
author of *The Platinum Rule* and *Charisma*

Acknowledgments

Nobody makes it alone, nobody. Even the guy (in 1958) who forced me to yell out "Popcorn . . . Peanuts!" as I and the other vendors climbed the steps of a football stadium helped me to sell better. It seems my timid approach wasn't letting enough of the fans know about my products. "Be proud of what you do," he said. "Yell it out!"

As I reflect on my fifty-plus years, I notice both profound and plain events that made me who I am. My gratitude goes out to all who have contributed.

Here are a few worthy of special note: Tony Alessandra, my best friend and former partner, helped me to understand professional marketing. Harold Gash sold me a library of tapes of Earl Nightingale and believed in me more than I did in myself.

Paula Cathcart, my wife of over three decades, whom I've been striving to impress since the day we met, has helped in more ways than she could know. Professional trainer and excellent father Jim Cathcart, Junior, gave me an enduring reason to be worthy of his admiration. My father, C. E. Cathcart, taught me personal accountability, with love.

Joe D. Willard gave me the opportunity to shine, long before I thought I was ready. Al Simensen, back in 1975, did not believe I was ready for advancement and therefore caused me to double my efforts to prove my value and potential.

Spencer Johnson, M.D., who I am sure will think this book covers too many ideas, taught me focus and challenged me to grow. Og Mandino once told his former boss, W. Clement

Stone, that I was a "great writer." Someday I hope to prove him right.

Two clients of special note are Peter Kutemann and Gary Goranson, who said that they wanted the people in their companies to think about business as I do.

And I'm grateful to the millions of people who have embraced the term "relationship selling" since I wrote the first book by that title in 1985. They have expanded the practice of this philosophy enormously.

Thank you all from the bottom of my heart. I promise to become ever more worthy of your gifts.

—Jim Cathcart
Lake Sherwood, CA, USA

How to Use This Book

Becoming a Relationship Selling Professional

I have divided this book into bite-sized pieces of information and arranged those pieces into eight major groupings called Competencies. A competency in this sense is a set of skills that help achieve the same overall goal. Each idea presented here is short enough to be studied and applied in merely fifteen minutes. There are enough ideas in this book to keep you growing for several years. Some ideas you will want to spend much time with, perhaps once or twice each year, others you might use only once.

The cumulative effect of studying and applying this information is that you will become worth more to your clients, your company, your industry and your own career. You will reach the top one percent of the people in your field. You will build "professional equity," a set of personal assets that give you clout and increase your potential for success.

Once you have read the first part of this book feel free to skip directly to the topics that are of most interest to you. With each idea written in a stand-alone style, you can navigate this book as you would a website, random access, the way you want to pursue it.

I have not focused on any one specific industry or type of selling (with the exception of an occasional example or illustration). In my speeches to companies around the world I have encountered just about every type of product and style of selling one could imagine. What I have found is that Relationship Selling works with all of them. Though specific applications may vary, the basic philosophy and overall skills needed are all the same.

Congratulations and thank you for purchasing this book. You are already on the road to becoming a top one percenter.

Good Selling!

Become the Person You Will Need to Be

The quickest way to assure that you receive something is to be sure that you are worthy of it and ready for it. I tell my seminar audiences, *"If you want something, then plan to deserve it."* So, how do you intentionally deserve something?

The answer is relatively simple; you focus on developing in yourself the qualities of a person who would deserve it. In other words, become the person you will need to be in order to achieve or receive what you desire.

The same process can apply to landing a large account. Ask yourself, what kind of person would probably land this account? What are the credentials they'd have? What personal qualities would they possess? How would they work with others? What special knowledge might they possess? Why would this client want them to be their sales representative or account executive? Then systematically acquire those traits.

Another approach to becoming the person you will need to be is to study those who are already enjoying the success you seek. Study the whole person when you can. Ask such questions as: Is this person fully successful or simply earning big money? What is the main impression others get from this person? What qualities stand out in him or her?

How does this person behave under stress? What do clients get from this person that they don't get from others? What has his or her path been? How did this person get to their current position? Then you can go and do likewise.

But remember, you are trying to become the best possible

you, not a newer version of this other person. It is *your* best that you want to achieve, not theirs. Emulation of others is helpful on some levels, but trying to be just like them will deny the greatness in you.

Ask yourself, "If I got all the breaks, did my very best, and truly applied myself, how good could I be?" The answer to that question is the picture of the person you will need to be.

Let's look at the eight areas in which top one percenters are effective: The Eight Competencies of Relationship Selling. This book is organized around those eight competencies. All the ideas, skill sessions, and exercises are categorized under one of these areas.

As you examine each area, ask yourself, "What do I need to know or do in order to be strong in this competency?"

1. **Preparation.** What skills or habits could you acquire in raising your sales readiness to its highest level?

2. **Targeting.** What resources, strategies, systems and habits could you cultivate to assure that you are always focused on the best prospects for your services?

3. **Connecting.** Which skills and traits could you cultivate that would cause others to want to do business with you?

4. **Assessing.** What qualities and expertise could you develop in order to be aware of not only what someone needs but also what they want?

5. **Solving.** Which attributes could you develop that would increase your ability to convince others to take the actions that were best for them?

6. **Committing.** What behaviors and processes could you encourage in you that would cause others to trust you enough to say "yes" and mean it?

7. **Assuring.** What processes could you implement that would make people remain satisfied with their decision to do business with you?

"You are the company's sales leader now, Peters.
You can use the regular door."

8. **Managing.** What systems, habits, resources and schedules could you put in place to assure that you were always doing well and consistently getting better as well?

Well over one hundred specific ideas and skills are contained herein, each designed to address at least one of the foregoing questions. Spend at least fifteen minutes each day on one of these ideas. The results will astound you.

Becoming the person you will need to be starts with knowing what you want and then systematically acquiring each skill or trait that will get you there. *You are already worthy of what you want; now all you have to do is become eligible for it, one skill at a time.*

"Everyone lives by selling something."

ROBERT LOUIS STEVENSON

The
Relationship
Selling Concept

How to Reach
the Top One Percent
of Your Field

WHAT IS IT THAT SEPARATES THE TOP PERFORMERS FROM THE REST?
That question has guided every success explorer since the beginning of personal achievement. It has myriad answers and none is *always* the right answer. The universal answer, of course, is "it depends." Each situation, industry, and person is unique.

Nevertheless, there are some things we can use as our guidelines. There are enough things in common across various industries that we can learn to navigate the upper regions of success in our fields.

The first thing is: *Nobody gets to the top one percent by luck or accident.*

Somebody may make a huge sale, or stumble into a great opportunity once in awhile, but staying there is very different. *When I say, "reach the top one percent," I mean reaching it and staking a lasting claim while you are there.* So, how do we distinguish the top one percent from everyone else?

The top one percent in any field are those who

- earn the most money (at the turn of the 21st century, the top one percent of wage earners in the United States were earning $373,000 a year or more).
- exert the most influence when they speak.
- receive the highest awards and recognition.
- are able to get major things done with minimal effort.
- set the pace and style for others.
- become the standard by which others are measured.

Here is what I have discovered, in my twenty-five years of professional speaking to over 2,400 organizations around the world, about "one percenters" and the characteristics they possess. One percenters:

- think differently about what they do. (They are building, not just doing.)
- build relationships in advance of needing them.
- take personal responsibility for making things happen.
- intelligently work the odds.
- intentionally form habits and cultivate patterns that work.
- know the payoffs of each of their activities.
- are impatient with those who don't take charge of their own lives and careers.
- are generous with their time and resources toward worthy recipients.

Those at the top understand that one must become and remain eligible for what they want. If you want the top people to seek you out, you must be the kind of person they would benefit from seeking out. If you

"I always suspected that the top producers
had a better break room."

want to be influential, you must continually learn more in order
to have more to offer.

Measure yourself against these characteristics. Then, as you
explore the eight competencies of sales leadership that follow,
look for ways to cultivate these qualities in your own life. The
good news is that it is within your grasp.

How to Produce Sales Right Now

Ask any salesperson or manager what they want most to know
about selling and their first question will likely be, "How do I produce sales right now?" The answer is: It depends upon whether
they care about making sales tomorrow as well.

3

To make sales today it would be easy to simply reduce your price until people say "yes." Or you could exaggerate the value of your product beyond your ability to deliver. In either case, people might buy today. But in both cases you would have problems tomorrow.

> The danger of transactional selling (short-term thinking):
>
> ## "They Buy Today, You Cry Tomorrow."

Or, you could consider that every "today" is a piece of "tomorrow." Without what you did yesterday, today wouldn't be the same.

Here is a quick formula for generating abundant sales right away without compromising your reputation, profitability, or long-term goals.

1. **Notice more.** Assess your current situation from many angles. Examine product, price, place, promotion, and people factors. Assess the eight competencies in yourself. What's working and what's not?

2. **Cover the gaps.** Assure stability in your delivery of value to those who buy. Get everyone's agreement to be accountable for doing their job well. Be sure you can be relied on to deliver what you promise.

3. **Increase human contact.** Make calls, send messages and e-mails, get others working with you, and be more visible.

4. **Begin a series of chain reactions.** Start the processes that result in sales, focus on steps one and two for now (but be ready to follow through).

5. **Keep the ball in your court.** Take initiative to follow through; don't rely on others to get back to you, call them.

6. **Maximize your leverage.** Use your best skills and resources, call on your best prospects, focus on your best products, and do good work during the prime selling hours. Spend at least fifteen minutes each day during non–prime time sharpening your sales skills.

7. **Think beyond today.** Remember that today's choices select tomorrow's challenges, so keep in mind your need to continue generating business in the future. Don't compromise your standards or tarnish your image.

CASE STUDY

Rancho Estrella, An Upscale Resort Hotel

Rancho Estrella, the Upscale Resort Hotel, is located in a suburban resort area near a major city. It has a long-term reputation as one of the finest properties of its type in the world. Its product is excellent: a recently renovated facility, highly trained and experienced staff, elegant dining, great location, luxurious accommodations, abundant recreational opportunities. Advertising has been very good, their public image is spotless and competitive positioning is good. All in all, you'd have to say they have a lot going for them.

Situation:

In recent months the economy has been weak and their occupancy levels (the number of rooms being booked per night) have been way down. The money they have for promotion is very limited. This problem is not unique to them; the entire hospitality industry has been experiencing the effects of reduced travel. But they have been selling fewer conventions and special events, so in addition to fewer individual travelers, they now have fewer groups using their hotel. Another upscale resort has been opened recently within a half hour's drive. News reports seem to indicate that it may be some time before the economy turns around and travel increases again.

What can they do to increase sales right now?

Small Tactics:

Here is the short-term thinking approach to increased profits:

• They could lower their rates, offer more amenities, and give away free meals or extra room-nights as an incentive to those who might book a room or event. They could also "lower their sights" to go after groups that normally couldn't afford this hotel. Though this might take business away from other hotels, and Rancho Estrella would make less profit on each sale, at least they would be making sales.

• Or, they could cut costs dramatically. Reduce the staff, close up the unused rooms, and reduce the hours of operation in the restaurants and bars. They could advertise less, discontinue their toll-free services and use regular toll calls for all promotions. They could freeze or reduce salaries and discontinue bonuses. Though this would discourage and frighten their employees, the short-term savings would be assured.

• Services that didn't directly produce revenue could be discontinued, such as evening turn-down service, free newspapers for frequent guests, free refreshments in the concierge lounge, and upscale amenity packages in guest suites. They could also buy less expensive furniture, bedding, towels, etc. All of these actions would reduce the cost of operations day to day in hopes of generating higher profits on the business they are already doing with people. Their costs would go down immediately but so would their visibility in the marketplace and the appeal of their resort to the guests.

• They could start new revenue sources by charging extra for valet parking and for local phone calls, and by discontinuing free refills on soft drinks, charging for the in-room coffee service, and charging extra for the use of premium TV channels. They could bill clients for the notepads in meeting rooms and charge a service fee for providing ice water in meetings. This would produce immediate income, but clients would be paying more just to get the same result and would quickly begin to resent the extra charges.

• In a final effort to generate sales today they could start a series of "sales blitz" events. This is where the sales team sets up a "boiler room" for massive phone calling. All the sales reps gather in one room at separate phones for hours on end, simply making one phone call after another in an effort to find a sale today. Each is given a list of potential prospects, or simply the yellow pages to call every person who might be a prospect for something their hotel sells. Yet another blitz could be a caravan of vehicles filled with sales reps combing the city to make cold calls on businesses and travel agencies in hopes of generating some sales. Their visibility would increase, but at what cost?

So, in light of the above, what do you think of Rancho Estrella's prospects for success now? Are they likely to weather the down economy and generate sales? Are they likely to gain the commitment of their staff to give an extra effort during the crunch? Will they rebound with the economy to their previous position of prestige, or will it take longer to recover? Will they still have the respect of their customers, colleagues, suppliers, employees and community? What do you think? Would you invest in them today?

Superior Strategies

Here is how a top one percenter, a Relationship Selling Professional, would approach this situation.

1. **Notice more**. A Relationship Selling Professional would begin by doing an inventory of assets. What is working well and how many good things do we have going for us? Next they would explore where today's business is coming from and why, and where the business came from in the recent past, and why. An analysis of the competitive situation would let us know who else might be trying the same things we decide to do, and who, among our competitors, is not being as intelligent about the situation. Further analysis could show where we are vulnerable and where our greatest voids exist. Each person needs to know which of the eight competencies they are strong in and where they need support. *The more we notice, the more we know. And the more we know, the more options we see. And the person with the most options usually wins.*

2. **Cover the gaps**. A Relationship Selling Professional would meet with our team of professionals and inform them of the situation, enlisting their support and seeking suggestions from all of them. Every person would tell their manager what results they are willing to be accountable for. Plans would be made to assure that any cutbacks did not show up

in a reduction of the quality of our product. Efforts would be made to include everybody in solving the problems so that morale stays high and performance quality does not suffer.

3. **Increase human contact**. The sales team would begin to have daily briefings. Short meetings in the morning and evening to plan and then review each day's activity. We want to assure that we are calling on our best prospects with our best sales strategies and that everyone works in concert so as to maximize our sales appeal. Each week acquires its own theme. One week is filled with an emphasis on e-mail messages, another is focused on in-person calls, another is about sending the best possible proposals, another is all about follow through. Though all these things are done each week, the alternating emphasis assures that we improve each effort to its optimum. Sales reps meet daily to give each other feedback on what they are doing well and how they can improve. New sales ideas are covered briefly each day. Positive attitudes are sustained and discouraging language is aggressively avoided.

4. **Begin a series of chain reactions**. The Relationship Selling Professional would initiate numerous new actions that are the first step in a new sales cycle. Inquiries would be sent out, prospective buyers and former customers would be interviewed. Proposals would be scheduled, presentations planned, meetings booked for sales calls and executive briefings, collaborations begun, and promises made. All of these are things that imply that more action will be taken later. All of them likewise give an impression of optimism and forward planning. *Not all sales can be generated by today's activity. Some of today's actions need to be sent ahead to prepare us for tomorrow's sales.*

5. **Keep the ball in your court**. The Relationship Selling Professional would not rely on callbacks from prospects. Calls and follow through would be initiated from our office

every day. Wall charts or computerized spreadsheets would be created to track who needs to contact whom and when. *Things that are measured tend to improve, so we would begin to measure and track every activity that contributes to a future sale.*

6. **Maximize your leverage**. The Relationship Selling Professional would block out the prime selling hours for only sales contacts. No letter writing, meetings, research or training would be done during the best hours for sales calls. All supportive activity would take place during times when prospects were hard to reach. Every department within the company would be informed of our efforts and encouraged to contribute in whatever way they can. All personnel would be told to "think sales" and appropriate rewards would be designed to thank them. Each person would spend fifteen minutes each day learning something new or sharpening a skill. Our suppliers and favorite customers would also be enlisted to help generate sales by building a fun-filled contest or campaign in which they could participate.

7. **Think beyond today**. People who can't envision a positive tomorrow are forced to assume it will not be positive. Therefore, a Relationship Selling Professional would assure that our leaders continually verbalized their optimism. Posters, memos, briefings, and training meetings would be filled with stories, examples, and images of the positive future possibilities. Optimism beats pessimism every time. (And yes, it beats "realism" too.)

How can you use the Rancho Estrella case study to apply to your own organization?

What are the similarities between Rancho Estrella and your company?

Which of these approaches to immediate sales have you tried lately?

Which would you prefer to try next time?

What changes are indicated in your current sales activities?
What other questions need to be asked to help your
organization grow?

**The benefit of Relationship Selling (longer-
term thinking):**

**They buy today and they buy again tomorrow . . .
and so do their friends.**

The Eight Competencies of Relationship Selling

*As a gymnast, almost every day, my goal was to train
about 15 more minutes than the rest of my teammates.
That little extra focus over a few years led to some
perfect 10's at the Olympic Games. Perfection does take
time . . . see what 15 minutes a day can do for you!*

PETER VIDMAR, Olympic champion, co-author,
Awaken the Olympian Within

*Sales is so basic that it cannot be considered a
separate function . . . it is the whole business seen from
the point of view of its final result, that is, from the
customer's point of view.*

PETER DRUCKER

*If you were to spend merely fifteen minutes each day gaining one new
sales idea or sharpening a skill, within just a few years you would become
an industry leader.* Sales excellence is acquired one skill at a time.

THE EIGHT COMPETENCIES OF RELATIONSHIP SELLING

I.

PREPARE TO SELL
Build and sustain sales readiness.

2.

TARGET THE RIGHT PROSPECTS
Identify who, how, and when to make contact.

3.

CONNECT WITH THE PERSON
Establish truthful communication, two ways.

4.

ASSESS THE NEEDS
Understand the needs of the person and their situation.

5.

SOLVE THE MAIN PROBLEM
Cause the person to experience the value you bring.

6.

COMMIT TO THE SALE
Confirm that a purchase has been made.

7.

ASSURE SATISFACTION
See that the customer remains satisfied with their decision.

8.

MANAGE YOUR SALES POTENTIAL
Lead, motivate and grow yourself.

The *Relationship Selling* philosophy is: Business should be practiced as an act of friendship, rather than merely as a process of negotiation. It is about connecting with people profitably, not just persuading them to buy.

I have organized the principles and practices of *Relationship Selling* within eight competencies, exhibited on the preceding page.

The pages that follow will provide you with the roadmap needed to build the kind of skills and relationships you must have in order to become a successful sales leader. The maxims put forth are not especially difficult. They do, however, require a new way of thinking and looking at yourself as a sales professional.

The Seven Steps of Relationship Selling

In the sales process, there are seven distinct steps that we go through; each corresponds with one of the competencies, leaving the *manage* competency as separate yet intertwined with all seven. The goal of each of these steps must be achieved in order to attain a successful sales relationship, a profitable outcome for both parties.

The first step in selling is getting ready to do your job really well. I call this *prepare*. Preparation is not simply sitting down and doing some paperwork, or gathering your notes together, or assembling your demonstration material, or plugging in your video player to give a demonstration video.

Preparing means handling all the things that must be prepared. For example, preparing your own attitude. Preparing the way you look, preparing to focus your attention on the client instead of thinking about something else. Preparing to be at the prospect's place of business at the time and location that works best for achieving a successful sale. *The ultimate goal of preparing is to be ready to do your job well.* Sometimes that takes a nanosecond— you're ready right now. Someone comes up to you and you say,

"A-ha! This is a prospect, I know what the person needs, I've talked with him before, I know what I need to tell him in order to make this sale. I'm ready right now." Yes, sometimes it only takes a second to prepare. Other times it takes days to prepare. "I need to go to their web site, I need to research information, I need to study up on the company. I need to check with a few people in the marketplace. I need to talk to some of their other suppliers. I need to find out what they've done in the past. I need to spend some time with them gathering a little information before I come back to them with a recommendation." In other words, sometimes preparation is a long-term thing, sometimes it's not. But in every case the goal is the same—be ready to do your job well.

The second step is *targeting*. This is where you assure that the people you go after, as prospects, are appropriate to your product and your goals. With the wrong target, you can attempt to sell all day long and still achieve only minimal results. Sure, you can sell refrigerators to Eskimos, but they are not your best prospects.

The next step is to *connect* with the person. This is the meeting phase of the sale, the connecting part. It is not just starting a dialogue, not just giving a pitch—it is establishing the kind of atmosphere in which they tell you the truth and you tell them the truth from the start.

Then, it is critical to understand them. You can call this studying, fact-finding, or any number of things, but the goal here is to understand them. I call this *assessing* the needs of both the person and their circumstances. *Until you understand the person, until you understand their situation, until you understand their needs, and their concerns, you're not ready to sell.*

Once you understand them, then you focus on *solving* for them. Solving their main problem, resolving their concerns, addressing their needs in such a way that you show them exactly what you can do for them to make their life better. Some people argue and say this is the "presentation," this is "the pitch." Well, that may be part of the experience, but the purpose of "solving" is for you to get *them* to understand what you can do for them. At first you want to understand them. Then you want them to understand you, to see the value you bring, to understand intellectually and to feel emotionally the ways you can serve them so that they feel compelled to commit.

That's the next step in the selling cycle—*commit*. Confirm the fact that a sale was made, a purchase was initiated. Do something to commit to the transaction between the two of you, the beginning of the relationship. *Until you get them to take an action, give you a handshake, sign a check, give you a purchase order, or do whatever people do to confirm their commitment to you, you don't have a sale, you simply have an interested prospect.* So the next step in selling is *commit*. And the purpose of that is to make the sale official.

The final step in selling, which starts the cycle once again, is *assuring* customer satisfaction. Assuring that this person who just said yes to you is indeed happy that they made that decision. Sometimes that means that not only do you need to reassure them verbally, but you also need to give them information that confirms and validates that this was a wise decision on their part. Sometimes it means giving them an orientation to the product, service or process they have now committed to. Sometimes it means introducing them to another person who will be there to provide the follow through. Sometimes it means providing a technical manual or giving them a DVD or a web address that allows them to gain more information to be sure that the guarantees and assurances you had given them will in fact be acted upon.

So, again, here are the seven steps in the sales process and the goal of each:

1. **Prepare.** The goal is to be ready to do your job well.

2. **Target.** The goal is to identify your best prospects.

3. **Connect.** The goal is to establish truthful communication, two ways.

4. **Assess.** The goal is to truly understand the person, the situation, and their needs.

5. **Solve.** The goal is to provide solutions, to get them to understand the value you bring to them.

6. **Commit.** The goal is to confirm the sale or the purchase, to make it official.

7. **Assure.** The goal is to make sure that this person truly sees, feels, and understands that what they did was a very good thing to do.

NOTE: The eighth competency—to *manage* yourself as a salesperson—is not a *step* in the sales process. Yet, unless you can continually manage and improve yourself, your sales success will be limited.

Your Sales Readiness Self-Assessment

The desire to win is meaningless without the will to prepare.

WINSTON CHURCHILL

The game is often won more fully during the practice sessions than simply within the contest.

JIM CATHCART

When we moved into our new home the previous tenants presented us with an aerial photo of the house and surrounding property. It gave us an entirely new perspective on our home and its placement in the neighborhood. Imagine if you could get that kind of perspective on your own readiness for selling. I believe you can.

Opposite is a diagram of an eight-spoked wheel, which shows all of the sales competencies, laid out in relation to each other. In this diagram, each spoke of the wheel represents one skill-set, one competency. The center of the wheel is the starting point and the outer ring of the wheel represents optimum development, a "ten."

By using each spoke as a self-rating scale, you can plot your current readiness in that area through placing a dot on the spoke indicating how ready you are in that competency today. If you feel that your "Prepare" competency is well developed at present, then you would place a dot near the outer ring, somewhere between an eight and a ten. If you feel less confident about your overall preparation readiness, then you would choose a rating closer to the center of the wheel, indicating a lower number.

After rating your "Prepare" competency, move on to the "Target" competency and repeat the process, selecting the number that you feel is most accurate today. Do this for all eight competencies.

Please resist the need to have a scientific assessment before doing this. What matters most for this exercise is for you to indicate where you think and feel you stand in each competency here and now, today. This is not a rating of your potential, nor is it an accurate objective assessment of your selling skills. It is merely an indicator of where you think you are. This produces what behavioral scientists call "face validity" for you. That means that you are telling yourself what you believe to be true.

By doing this you will portray graphically what you now merely know intellectually or emotionally. This produces a self-portrait from the perspective of an overview, or aerial snapshot so to speak.

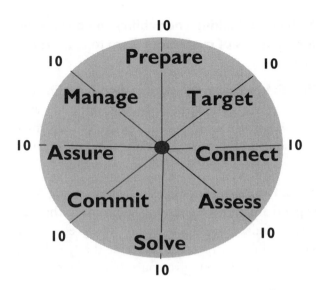

Your Sales Readiness Profile

Use these questions to help select the number that applies to each rating today. How ready are you for selling? There are eight elements in the sales process. Think about yourself in each of these. What is your current level of competence or effectiveness in the following?

■ **PREPARE: Sales planning and preparation.** How good are you at being ready to do your job well? On a scale of zero to ten (zero being low, ten being high) think about how ready you are, how competent and effective you are in sales planning and preparation. Write the number down, zero to ten.

■ **TARGET: Prospecting.** How ready are you for prospecting, how well do you identify the people who might want what you have, and find a way to get in touch with them? Also, what about your quantity? That's the number of new sales contacts that you make. On a zero-to-ten scale, include in this ranking how many new calls and contacts you make, say in a typical week. Give yourself a ranking.

■ **CONNECT: Ranking your ability to connect with all different types of customers.** Zero to ten, write down a number.

■ **ASSESS: Interviewing and fact-finding skills.** How good are you at asking questions and listening well to draw out the answers? How about in finding the kind of information about the person and the situation that makes you as effective as you could be? Zero to ten, write down a number.

■ **SOLVE: Problem solving.** How about solving the problem, how good are you at presenting solutions to the customer so that they understand? How well do you present your ideas? How well do you dramatize the value that you bring to someone? Zero to ten, give yourself a ranking.

■ **COMMIT: Confirming the purchase, getting a commitment, closing the sale.** How good are you at asking for the order, and asking in such a way that the person wants to say yes? How good are you at overcoming the resistance that you meet, eliminating resistance in the first place, and getting the person comfortable with making a commitment to you, today? Zero to ten, write down your response.

■ **ASSURE: After-sale communication and follow through.** Is the customer satisfied with what they got from you? How good are you at the after-sale communication? And, how good are you at staying in touch and following through to see to it that that customer is truly happy that they got what they wanted and needed in a way that they understand and value? Rate your current level of competence or effectiveness in that area. Zero to ten.

■ **MANAGE: Managing yourself as a salesperson.** How effective, how competent are you at keeping yourself motivated, keeping yourself skilled, keeping yourself in a learning mode so that you're constantly getting better and becoming worth more to your company, to your customer, and to your own personal career? Choose a number.

You've just looked at eight areas—sales planning and preparation, prospecting, and the quantity of new sales calls, interviewing, understanding the customer, presenting solutions to customers, confirming the purchase, after-sale follow through, and managing yourself as a salesperson. On the zero-to-ten scale, you chose a ranking for each of those eight areas.

Now, add those together. Get the total number of all your rankings. Then divide it by eight. See what the norm is, see the average of your response. That will tell you your overall sales readiness at this point in your life, today; write that number here _____. Today's date is _____.

If you want to know how to get better, look at each individual ranking and think about what you could do to move it from a zero to a one, or a one to a five, or a six to a ten. To improve yourself in each of the vital areas of sales effectiveness, focus on each one individually.

And, periodically, do this self-assessment again and date it. Keep a running account of your overall and your specific sales readiness.

Plotting Your Rankings on the Chart

Once you have placed a dot on each spoke, take a moment to connect each of these dots, one to another, around the wheel. (Do this in pencil or on separate paper, because you will want to do it again at other times.) The result of your connect-the-dots exercise will produce a figure within the wheel. If your ratings are all at the same number, say all sevens, then your figure within the wheel will be a wheel that is seven-tenths the size of the overall wheel. But most people don't end up with consistent ratings in all of the competencies. Where one rating might be a ten, another may be a three or a five. This produces a strangely shaped figure inside the wheel illustrating differences in readiness for each competency.

Note in which competencies you feel the most readiness and in which you feel the least. Use this awareness to consider which aspects of this book on Relationship Selling you need to focus on the most right now. You may need more work in connecting with people than you do in targeting the right prospects. Or you may feel strong in assuring satisfaction after the purchase but not as strong in managing yourself as a salesperson. Whatever result you have indicated, it tells you something important. It tells you where you think you need the most and least support or extra work.

It has been said that a self-assessment is not as objective as a third-party assessment, but then again, objectivity is only half the picture. If you were judged by experts to have excellent readiness for assessing a customer's needs but you didn't feel confident in that area, chances are strong that your performance wouldn't be optimum in that area. Your self-doubt would show in the way you communicated with the prospects. On the other hand, if you were really doing a good job of managing yourself as a salesperson, your results in many areas would be good despite any lack of confidence in the same category.

So both views are needed, internal and external.

Let this aerial view of your sales readiness begin the process of exploring how you are strong and where you need more resources, for now.

Self-awareness is the first step toward self-control and self-improvement.

What Is Missing from Your Sales Arsenal?

Nothing happens until somebody sells something.

ARTHUR "RED" MOTLEY

Only about one percent of the people who read this book will do so simply to get better at selling. Most of the readers will be seeking a specific answer; a solution to some aspect of selling that has eluded them. Where they find that answer in this book will vary based on where they are in their own professional development. What may seem irrelevant today may be just the answer that is needed tomorrow.

To determine which aspect of selling might be holding you back, explore the following eight questions. If you are missing sales, is it due to the following:

1. Not knowing enough about your product, your competition, your industry or your customers? (Focus on the Prepare competency.)

2. Calling on people who are not good prospects for you? Could it be that you are not making enough calls? (Focus on the Target competency.)

3. Difficulty in getting people to open up to you and tell you what you need to know? (Focus on the Connect competency.)

4. Not knowing the customer's real needs or motives? (Focus on the Assess competency.)

5. Customers not understanding how much benefit they will gain from doing business with you? (Focus on the Solve competency.)

6. An inability to get customers to make a commitment to buy? (Focus on the Commit competency.)

7. Having sales fall apart or having customers leave you for another supplier? (Focus on the Assure competency.)

8. Difficulty in keeping yourself motivated to sell, or to find the time needed to do your work? (Focus on the Manage competency.)

Your answers will vary based on when you ask yourself these questions. So go to the specific parts of this book that are relevant to your immediate needs. Find the answers and get some results today! Later you can explore the other topics and sharpen all your sales skills.

Spend at least fifteen extra minutes each day improving one aspect of your selling skills.

The Evolution of Sales Practices

Relationship Selling. What does that really mean? Does it mean you put all the emphasis on the relationship? Or do you still keep some emphasis on the sale? Moreover, what's the difference between what might be called traditional selling and *Relationship Selling?*

To answer these questions, let's put things in context. My son was born in the year 1971. My grandson was born in the year 2001. Let's look at the difference in how selling was done a generation ago versus how selling is done today.

A generation ago, selling was done primarily with cold calls. People went out, unannounced, showed up on somebody's doorstep or in their foyer and announced that they wanted a couple of minutes of their time so that they could make a sales presentation. Such a way of selling was not only common, it was expected.

What made the salesperson effective was a strong sales pitch. The best salesperson could tell their story in a convincing and compelling way. They were hard closers. Good salespeople had all kinds of power-closing techniques. They had the "nail-down," the "half-nelson close," the "hat-in-hand close," and the "sharp-angle close." All of these supposed "friendship building" techniques were designed to manipulate someone into a position of submission so they had to say, "Yes!"

This was possible because most buyers were uninformed. Buyers simply didn't know about the products because information was not available to everyone as it is today.

What's different today? Today with e-mail, with the World Wide Web, with universal access to people and information by telephone and computer and otherwise, we have an enormously different marketplace. We've got a marketplace of informed

buyers, people who are much more sophisticated and aware than ever before. They will not tolerate cold calls in the traditional sense, strong sales pitches followed by hard closing and so forth. *People today expect the salesperson to be an expert guide, a consultant, and most of all a business friend:* someone who will be there after the sale to assure that they get full value from the decision that they made to commit to doing business with you.

In the old days, if you were a strong persuader, you had a future in sales. Presently, that's only one tiny element in the overall mix of talents and skills that you need. Today, the best selling skills you can develop are the skills that constitute a package of what we might call consulting skills. Those are built on the assumption that there will be a business relationship established, that the business relationship will endure beyond the transaction of this sale and that the consultant will determine needs before just prescribing solutions.

There's a line that sales trainers have used for years: *"Selling is like medicine, prescription without diagnosis is malpractice."* If you start selling before you fully understand the person you're selling to, then you're being inappropriate and you're being ineffective. You could be a far better salesperson by first understanding their needs and then addressing them.

So *Relationship Selling*, the way it's done today, is a matter of professional behavior, applied to the cultivation of relationships, which generate profitability for you and your company and profitability for the person who decided to do business with you. They profit from the value you bring. You profit from the revenue that they provide.

Solutions and Connections

Society advances based on two things: the solutions we produce, and the connections we sustain. If we produce the right kind of solutions to people's needs and problems, then society advances. But that's not all that causes it to advance. If all we had were technology, things would pretty soon reach a standstill because they would be lacking the other element.

The other element is connections. The connections with each other, the connections between suppliers and buyers, the connections between us and the other people in our community and in our marketplace and within our own profession. Those connections are also what cause business to advance, together with the solutions.

The same thing is true for your sales career. Your sales career will advance based on the quality and quantity of solutions you provide to people, and the quality and quantity of connections you sustain. *We used to say, "It's not what you know, it's who you know."*

In actuality, it's more: It's who cares whether they know you. It's not just the people you know, but it's the people you've actually formed a connection with, a meaningful relationship with. That's what helps advance your career.

There used to be a statement widely used in marketing and sales, and that was, "Build a better mousetrap and the world will beat a pathway to your door." The belief was that if you had good technology, a good product or service, people would find you. That was probably true in the days when there were very few good solutions available. But today, there is a plethora of good solutions. They are everywhere. Today the choice is no longer between a bad product and a good product. It's in finding all these good products and knowing which one is the right one for you.

Think of automobiles back in the '50s, the heyday of big cars. We had the cars with fins and big menacing-looking grills, and loud pipes coming out the back, and huge V8 engines under the hood. However, those automobiles left oil slicks on our driveways. They needed frequent tune-ups. Sparkplugs frequently got fouled and had to be replaced. And, many of them were hard to drive.

Today we have automobiles of which even the least expensive sometimes will go 100,000 miles without a tune-up.

Technology has advanced so much that our biggest problem is choosing between good alternatives, not simply identifying the bad versus the good.

Ask yourself, since society is going to advance based on the solutions we produce and the connections we sustain, what can you do to cultivate even better connections with the key people in your world? And what can you do to constantly refine, advance, and enhance the solutions that you provide to people's problems?

Industrial Era versus Organic Era Selling

In the industrial era, we looked at business as a machine. As a matter of fact, we looked at the entire world as a machine. Everything was considered to operate by mechanical principles and we used physics as the primary science that guided us.

"They're extinct in nature, but a few still exist in the corporate world."

In the old mechanical paradigm, there was really no reason to think about the feelings of the machine. There was no reason to care about what went on after the sale as long as the sale was profitable and the customer got what he or she was buying.

Today we recognize that we do not live in a mechanical world. We live in a world that is biological. Therefore, we are entering what could be called the organic era.

We have started realizing that a business or an organization is a living entity. A business is alive. A community is alive. A church is alive. And, a network of people is alive. If you don't believe that, just identify one and sit back and study it for awhile.

If organizations and groups of people are living systems, then using physics as our way of studying them is quite limiting. What we should use instead is biology. In physics you reduce everything to the simplest, smallest element and then you manipulate those elements in an effort to create the desired mechanical result.

In biology, you begin with the assumptions that not only are the elements in existence, but they live and operate within an ecosystem. The environment, the marketplace, the overall community is a daily part of the experience that that person, that company, that product, that group of people will have.

What does that mean to you as a salesperson? It means that you must look at the companies you call on and the individuals you work with as being part of a living network. It compels you to recognize that nobody is alone, that everything you do or they do out there, affects something else.

Therefore, simply negotiating with people to get them to say yes is grossly inadequate. What we need to do today is to approach every business relationship as the beginning of a business friendship—an act of friendship that we are doing toward them to make their life better.

Industrial vs. Eco-Tech

• Mechanisms	• Organisms
• 9 to 5	• 24/7
• Formal Education	• Perpetual Education
• Eye Contact	• E/Contact
• IQ	• EQ
• Knowledge Is Power	• Access Is Power
• Persuasion	• Partnering
• Keep Up	• Stay in the Game
• Do It Yourself	• Do It Together
• Institutions Rule	• Individuals Rule

Your Edge: Product, Price, and People

Have you ever gone out to buy something, found what you were looking for, at a reasonable price, and yet you refused to buy it because you didn't like the way the person was selling it? I've asked that question of thousands of audiences over the years, and every single time, most of the people raise their hand with a "Yes."

Sometimes it's not your product or price that determines whether you get the business. Sometimes it's simply the way you connect with people. In the final analysis, after the sale is made, after the products or services are delivered and the person has committed to the purchase, the only thing that truly remains is the relationship between the seller and the buyer.

What makes someone buy from a particular company or salesperson? In many cases the reason is neither the product, nor the price, but rather the relationship with the individual they're dealing with. Products change, services change, prices change, certainly the economy and marketplace change. But when the relationship is strong, the account endures.

When you don't have an edge in product or price, then you must have an edge in the way you connect with people. In fact, you need that edge even if you do have a competitive product, or a price advantage. So always look for ways to value the relationship and recognize in your own mind that the relationship is the source for the sale. *When you connect with people, you not only get the business from today's transaction, you get the business from tomorrow's transactions as well.*

The Five P's of Marketing

Back in the Industrial Era, when we taught marketing, we would teach people the four P's: Product, Price, Place, and Promotion. If you have the right product, at the right price, in the right place, with the right promotion, you will be successful . . . or so we thought.

Well, that works pretty well until you think beyond the initial sale. If you start thinking beyond the initial sale, you recognize that one of the primary keys to the whole marketing mix is the individual, the human factor.

So we might add a fifth P to this mix: Product, Price, Place, Promotion and *Person, or People*, if you prefer. Almost every marketing class still teaches the "Four P's of Marketing," but today, more and more of them have come to recognize that success comes from the right person, with the right qualities, being in the right place, with the right price, the right product, and right promotion.

So think about marketing and how you can add yourself to that mix in such a way that you expand the possibilities.

Look at the Five P's. Which one do you need to work on most right now? Do you need to work on yourself, to increase your skill as a salesperson? Do you need to work on improving your product or your offering so that you have more value to bring to the person who buys? Do you need to look at your price, and find creative ways to present or alter your price, so that it's more appropriate to the market or person who's buying it? Do you need to examine the place from which you're marketing, the locations, the ease of access? Do you need to look at how you're accessible online or how you're accessible geographically to make it easier for people to buy from you? Or do you need to look at your promotion to see what kind of brand identity you're projecting into the marketplace? Which is it you need to work on most right now? Product? Price? Place? Promotion? Or People?

The Relationship or The Sale

Relationship Selling. Which word is more important? The relationship? Or the selling?

I've asked that question of many audiences and typically they'll say, "It's the relationship that's the most important."

If you build a good relationship with somebody in business, and you never make a sale, what's that worth to you in round numbers? Zero. In other words, the relationship without the sale is not worth much.

On the other hand, what if you make a sale to someone, but you do it in such a way that you don't cultivate a relationship with him or her? How hard is the second sale going to be? Not only as hard as the first, it will be harder than the first. People today expect that we will be professionals in selling. They expect that we will connect with them and be their business friend, that we will be there for them to see to it that they get what they bought, that the product or service is delivered with integrity, and that the decision they made to do business with us turns out to be a solid business decision.

The relationship matters and the sale matters. It's not a matter of either/or; it is one phrase—*Relationship Selling*—that describes a way of going about making sales, building relationships and cultivating profitable, ongoing connections with people.

In the decade or two just after World War II, salespeople perfected what we now call the Traditional Selling Approach. This approach relied heavily on a great opening pitch and a strong, powerful close. It was largely one-sided, the salesperson didn't take much time to understand the prospect, didn't care about his or her needs. Instead they "created" needs. The prospect learned a great deal about the salesperson's product because it was all the salesperson doing the presenting, the prospect listening. Then the prospect would decide whether or not to buy. Of course, if they resisted buying, the salesperson had dozens of ways of overcoming that resistance.

Selling today is more about relationships, about connections with people. Prospects are choosy. They won't waste a lot of time on unfocused sales pitches or old-fashioned notions. They want to develop a useful, professional relationship with salespeople and suppliers who can help them solve problems and help them answer questions.

In *Relationship Selling*, the salesperson takes time up front to build a sincere, committed relationship; they do this by investing time in learning about the customer's needs. Every step of the sales process that follows is conducted with that relationship primarily in mind.

What we're looking for when we go out to connect with someone is to build a relationship, which is based on the assumption that we're at the same time generating sales. *Relationship Selling is about making sales while building relationships.*

■ ■ ■

The Eight Competencies of Relationship Selling

THE FIRST COMPETENCY

Prepare
Build and Sustain
Your Sales Readiness

Be Ready to Do Your Job Well

WHEN IT COMES TO PREPARING FOR THE SALES CONTACT—being ready to do your job really well—there are several areas to think about.

First, preparing your prospect knowledge, researching your prospects, finding out who they are, where they are, what they need and how they think.

Next, rehearsing the sales contact. That's one of the most overlooked areas in selling. A lot of salespeople will think about what they're going to do, but seldom do they think it through as if it were actually happening. I've found that one of the most powerful things we can do is to role play either live with another person or in our mind exactly what's likely to happen in the ideal sales contact. Think about the person you're calling on and then see the sales call unfold in your mind.

Next, "reloading," or reviewing your previous notes and gathering your background information so that you really are ready, mentally, to have the facts you need in the front of your mind. Refreshing your knowledge about your own products and services. Do you regularly "reload the database" in your head? If so, what do you do for that? In other words, *how do you get the information you already know from the depths of your memory to the top of your awareness?*

Next is anticipating what this particular customer might need or want. Thinking from their point of view, what is it they need in relation to what you do? What about their wants? And what about the feelings they have?

Next, anticipating potential concerns or objections: What is it they might be bothered about, or concerned about? What kind of things would cause them to resist saying "yes" to you today?

Next, visualizing your desired sales results. Think it through and get to the end of the sales contact and think, what is the outcome I really want? What would that look like? What would it sound like? What would it feel like? How can I see that in my own head happening in reality, so that when I get there, it actually takes place?

Next, seeking coaching from someone else, such as a sales manager or an immediate supervisor, or a leader upline from you. Do you seek out other people's coaching? If so, how do you do that and how could you do it more effectively?

Then, anticipating the next steps. Thinking beyond the sale—what will happen after the sale, *once this person says "yes," what happens next? How can I be ready for that?* How can I help them be ready for that?

Next, preparing yourself with a variety of specific, thirty-second sales messages—little sound bites of ideas that you can present, one at a time, or all strung together. *When someone asks you a question, you should have a series of micro presentations already thought through in your mind, so that you can instantly describe, in the way you'd like to, the benefit or value that you want to convey to the customer.*

Next, your own awareness and skill level as it relates to your products and services. Not just knowing about your products and services, but also being able to use, or apply, or illustrate what value your product or service brings to someone, because you've practiced it, you've seen it in action, you've recently refreshed your awareness of this. A clumsy demonstration can spoil a sales opportunity.

Next, your current level of awareness of your competitor's products or services, and their features and benefits. Knowing how you stack up to the other options that are available to your customers.

And, finally, your own frame of mind. Get yourself thinking good thoughts about your product, your prospect, and yourself. It always shows on some level, so bring good energy to the sales call.

In each of these areas, as you prepare for a sales contact, if you have refreshed and renewed and sharpened your skills in each area, you truly will be ready to do your job well.

Preparing Yourself to Excel

We are all continually faced with a series of great opportunities brilliantly disguised as insoluble problems.

JOHN W. GARDINER

The trouble with opportunity is that it often arrives in overalls and looks like hard work.

THOMAS A. EDISON

There's quite a difference between merely being prepared and being prepared to excel. For one, all that is expected of you is competence. For the other, you are expected to achieve excellence. So, what does it take to be prepared for excellence?

It takes the right knowledge, the right information, the right resources, the right skills, the right physical readiness, the right attitude, and the right circumstances. Another way of looking at it is: You need a clear target, the tools to do your best, the training to use the tools fully, the time to prepare, the truth about what is going on, the checkpoints for tracking your progress, the "touch" or interaction with others who can help, and the trust of others which allows you to use your own good judgment.

Try this checklist before each sales contact:

1. How ready am I to do this task well?
2. Do I know what I need to know for this call?
3. What information that I may already know should I review in order to "reload my database" for instant awareness and responsiveness when needed?
4. Have I reviewed the customer's public information (brochures, website, annual report) so that I know what I should before this contact?
5. Do I have the resources and tools I will need to do this call professionally and well?
6. Have I sharpened the skills that will make me excellent at this?
7. Am I rested or warmed up enough to be at my best physically?
8. Am I groomed and dressed appropriately for the impression I want to convey?
9. Have I gotten into the right frame of mind for a successful outcome?
10. Is my attitude toward myself positive?
11. Is my attitude toward my customer respectful and positive?

12. Is my attitude toward my company, industry and competition strong and appropriate?

13. Have I created or chosen the right circumstances for this contact?

14. Have I visualized the outcome I want from this contact?

With this questionnaire you can identify any neglected areas that might trip you up on a sales contact. Once these self-check questions become second nature to you, your sales readiness will remain much higher.

Assessing Your Professional Equity

I'd like to introduce you to a concept I've developed over several years. I call it *Professional Equity*. When we use the term *equity*, typically we either think about fairness and balance or we think about ownership. In real estate terms, equity means the degree to which you've removed encumbrances, like mortgages, and acquired ownership.

Well, in your sales career, in your professional life, you also build equity. Equity is an important concept, which deals with the degree to which you have removed the encumbrances to your career and opened up your possibilities for achievement.

Here are some of the professional assets that constitute your professional equity:

- Your reputation
- Your credentials
- Your relationships or connections
- Your education
- Your depth and breadth of product knowledge
- Your professional background experience
- Your level of skill
- Your personal wealth

Each of the assets that you build eliminates a liability that could inhibit your career growth. Together these assets constitute your professional equity.

If you want to reach the top one percent of your field, the quickest way to do it is to build your professional equity, to cultivate the qualities, the skills, the experiences, and the connections that will take you to the top of your field.

Let's take a moment to assess how much equity you've built in your sales career. On a one-to-ten scale, rate yourself in the following areas (ten indicating you're at an optimal level of achievement in that category, at this point in your sales career, and one indicating you're at the bottom of that category at this point in your sales career).

For best results, do this exercise twice. First, do it by yourself to see how you think about your level of professional equity and your skills. Then, do it again later with a partner to uncover how others perceive your strengths or needs. Ask a trusted friend or a manager to rate you in these areas and then discuss the results of your rating and their rating.

Determine the implications of your scores in each area and see what you can do to advance your professional maturity, build more professional equity in each. *Sometimes a small increase in one of these areas will add up to a major advancement in your career.*

Again, write down a number from one to ten, as to where you think you are right now in the following categories:

- Your professional credentials
- Your on-the-job experience
- Your professional maturity
- Your interpersonal skills, your ability to relate to people
- Your self-management skills, getting yourself to do what needs to be done
- Your professional appearance, how you present yourself, how you look

■ Your professional demeanor, how you carry yourself

■ Your social skill, your ability to interact with various people, to perform effectively in a social situation

■ Your breadth of knowledge, the number of things that you know about in general

■ Your specifically industry-focused expertise and knowledge, your depth of knowledge in one particular area.

■ Your relationships or connections with influential people in your field

■ Your vocabulary, your ability to articulate and communicate

■ Your knowledge and awareness of business trends, community trends, and marketplace trends

Look back over your numbers. What you've done is not an evaluation of the facts, but rather an observation of your opinions. This is not necessarily where you actually are in your career, but it is a very accurate evaluation of your perception of where you are right now.

Some people say, "Where I am is where others think I am." Maybe they're right. Some people say, "Where others think I am is not necessarily the truth." Maybe they're right too. I think it was Willard Gaylin, a psychologist, who said, "Who we appear to be may not be who we actually are. But who we appear to be is definitely an important part of who we actually are." So both your perception and the perceptions of others count.

The next step is to sit down with someone else in the know to compare your rankings with their rankings of you. Then talk about what you need to do; or if you don't feel comfortable talking with them about it, think about it on your own. What do you need to do to advance each one of these items on the scale? As you go on, you'll be building professional equity, and sometimes one small improvement will make one very large success advancement.

An opportunity is only an opportunity if you are ready for it.
So how can you increase the number of things you are ready
for? By building your professional equity. Become an "eligible
receiver."

**Know your strengths, that's the important thing. You've
got to know what you are good at.**

<small>PETER DRUCKER, in answering interviewer Bill Moyers' question
as to what he would tell young adults in the 21st Century.</small>

How Do You Want to Be Known?

If other people were talking about you in a favorable way, what
would you want them to say, ideally? How would you like them
to describe you to each other?

Imagine for a moment that you could mold the way others
think and talk about you. Using the following sentence as a
prompt, describe yourself as you wish others would describe you.
"He or she is a person who _____." Or try this one:
"The way I feel toward him or her is _____." Here's
an example: "She's a person who truly cares about her customer,
who takes pride in her work, who is trustworthy and enjoyable
to be with. A person I admire and would like to learn from. I feel
that she is someone I trust to do a thorough job. Someone I look
forward to meeting again. And someone who will continue to
have a highly successful sales career."

Wouldn't you like to have someone say those kinds of things
about you? Well, you actually can. You determine how others
talk about you. You're in charge of how you're known by other
people. No, you don't control it completely; you don't have one
hundred percent control. But you clearly influence the way others think about you every day through your choice of how you
look, what you know, how you dress, how you present yourself,

how you perform on the job, how you follow through, how you relate to people, and how you manage yourself.

I recommend that you engage in "reputation management." Anyone can build and deserve the reputation they want over time.

So how do you want to be known? When you've described the ideal you in your own journal or personal notes—the way you would like others to think about you, talk about you, feel toward you—then you can cultivate in yourself the qualities that make you worthy of that description. The more you build those qualities in yourself, the more likely you are to hear someone else saying those things about you.

Try this exercise: Write out in one or two sentences exactly what you would like others to think, feel and say about you in the following categories. Be specific, as if you were putting the actual words in their mouths. To make this easier, think in terms of what you would like them to say about you three to five years from now.

Your friends
Your family members
Your coworkers
Your colleagues
Your industry
Your competitors
Your community

The statements you write out for each of these categories can probably be reduced into one overall paragraph that applies to all of them. Once you have refined the "reputation" statement into a few short sentences, write it on a separate card or sheet of paper and review it every day. In the morning and again in the evening, look at the card and read the reputation you wish to earn. In a short time you will begin to deserve it, and over time you will have it in reality. Take charge of your future by building the reputation you want.

When he began to use his nickname
Theodore seemed more approachable.

The Daily Question

Anyone who has ever heard me give a keynote speech at a big conference has probably heard me share the story about meeting a young man named Tim Seward.

Tim Seward came to a seminar that I was doing in Chicago in 1979, when he was 19 years old and had just begun his new business in the field of auto detailing, cleaning and polishing cars. At the end of that seminar, Tim came to me and asked if I could give him an idea or a slogan that he could use for daily motivation to keep himself on track in achieving his sales goals.

I first inquired of Tim, "What are your sales goals?"

He said, "I want to be the international sales leader for my company."

Impressed with his goal, I told him to do the following every day when he woke up: *"Ask yourself this question: How would the person I'd like to be do the things I'm about to do?"*

He said, "What do you mean?"

I said, "Think about your goal of being the international sales leader. How would the international sales leader start his day? How would the international sales leader dress? How would the international sales leader solve problems and work with customers and react to challenges that came up?"

Happily, he said, "I've got it, I've got it!"

So Tim went back home to Bay City, Michigan, and went to work on the idea of becoming the international sales leader. He knew that at the end of the year the person who became international sales leader would get to go to New Orleans to the international convention and would win a white Corvette.

Tim went to the local Chevrolet dealer in Bay City, Michigan, and got a photograph of a Corvette out of one of their brochures, took it home, put it over the workbench in his garage and put another one over his bed.

That year the Corvettes pictured in the brochures were blue, so he painted his white and had it hanging there. He looked at it every day and he asked himself, with this in mind as his prize, "How would the international sales leader do what I'm about to do?"

He changed the way he dressed, got rid of the t-shirt and jeans, got a professional looking jumpsuit that said "Tim" on the pocket and had his company name on the back. As he went about his work, he did a little bit more for each customer than he had done in the past, thinking the international sales leader would probably be the kind of person who would be gracious and do more than people expected from him. He also organized his files a little better, did more follow through on each sales lead and handled his business in a more professional manner.

By the time New Orleans rolled around, when they were having the international convention, I had been called to come and give a speech. Tim in the meantime knew that he had achieved several goals. His business had grown so much he had to hire other people to help him. He had to lease a service station so he'd have a permanent location from which to do business.

His business continued to grow, and he knew in going to New Orleans that he was eligible to win the award of international sales leader, but he didn't know if he had won it.

In New Orleans, when I gave my speech, we were in the grand ballroom. There was a great stage, and on the stage was a white Corvette with little spotlights shining all over it. The people were seated at tables with elegant tablecloths, and candles, and steak and lobster—just a very delightful evening.

At the end of my speech, the president of the company, Gary Goranson, stepped forward to announce the winner of the competition.

He said, "This year, we have had an amazing competition. The person who finished second led the person in third place by only one point. Third led fourth by one point. Fourth led fifth by two points. Fifth led six by one point. It was a tight competition . . . except for first place. The person in first place led the competition by over 300 points! There was no competition for first place, we have a clear winner. Ladies and gentlemen, welcome with me, from Bay City, Michigan, your International Sales Leader, Tim Seward!"

The place went insane, people jumped up and screamed, and cheered, started hugging each other, dancing around the room. Music was playing, and with spotlights sweeping the group, they brought Tim on their shoulders to the platform where he stood and stroked the Corvette.

I walked over and gave him a big hug of congratulations and I said, "What in the world did you do?"

He said, "I just did what you said to do back in Chicago."

I asked, with a grin, "What specifically might that be?"

He said, "Jim, come on, I'm talking about the daily question. How would the person I'd like to be do the thing I'm about to do?"

Twenty years later, I saw Tim in Ft. Myers, Florida, where he drove me from Ft. Myers Airport to his home in Southern Florida. We had dinner by his indoor pool with his wife and son.

He told me about his new life.

He said, "Jim, I sold my business detailing cars to another individual and then I built another company and I sold that. Then I built another company and I just sold that one for seven million dollars. And I'm retired now at age 38."

Age 38. He retired, managing his investments and enrolled in a local college where he was taking courses to get his MBA. When he was not doing those two things, he was flying around the world, taking his wife and son to places they never dreamed they'd ever be able to see. Tim is phenomenally successful. He's young. He's an industry leader. He has built and sold companies. And now, he is very, very wealthy.

I said to him, "Tim, I have just one question. Do you have a quote, or a slogan, or a motto you could give me as a daily motivator?"

He laughed and said, "I sure do. Ask yourself every day, how would the person I'd like to be do the things I'm about to do?"*

Need for Product Knowledge versus Selling Skill

What do you need to do to be ready to make a sale?

Years ago, I worked as a sales consultant to an insurance agency. I had a group of estate planners and insurance agents who were my team—my charges, if you will. And my job was to

---

*This story is also shared in my book *The Acorn Principle* (see Recommended Reading, page 239 of this book).

work with this group of people to cultivate their sales ability and to keep them motivated—self-motivated, not motivated by me—to be out in the community making sales, generating business, and building the reputation of that insurance agency.

Once, we were having a sales training meeting and one of the agents said to me, "I'm not making enough sales calls, and I'm certainly not making enough sales."

And I said, "Those two would kind of go hand in hand."

He said, "Yeah, but what I really need is more product knowledge."

Now this was a guy who already did have a lot of product knowledge. He was a very savvy salesperson and a subject matter expert when it came to the products he was representing. *But his lack of confidence, he thought, came from a lack of product knowledge. In actuality, it came from a lack of selling skill and a lack of customer knowledge.*

So what we did was focus on practicing, role playing, some selling skills that would allow him to know more clearly what he was going to do when he talked with a prospect, how he was going to present his ideas, and how he was going to gather information from them. We put special emphasis on what he needed to know about each person in order to prescribe the right solutions and make their life better.

When you're preparing for a sales contact, the way to build your confidence and increase your readiness is to know your customer, know your company, know your product, know your market, know your competitor, and know yourself. It is more important to know your customer than to know your product.

It is not important to know the answer to every question a prospect might ask. What is important is to build confidence that comes from knowing how to find the right solution for each prospect. Out of your confidence, their trust will grow and resistance to buying will disappear.

The Sales Planning Guide

The Importance of Planning

Historians readily agree that General Dwight David Eisenhower was one of the most successful military commanders of the last two-hundred years. His ability to organize a plan led directly to many decisive victories by the Allies in World War II. When asked the importance of planning by a reporter after the landings at Normandy on D-Day, Eisenhower said matter-of-factly, "Plans are nothing; planning is everything."

I suggest that you regularly use a sales planning guide. Before you call on an account, you have to have a purpose for the call, of course, and it can be as simple as calling to confirm that a delivery arrived on time, or as complex as meeting face-to-face for an information-gathering session. But you've got to have a purpose for the call.

So no matter what the reason, the more organized you are, the greater your chances of achieving your objective. Here are some questions that you can keep in mind for each sales call that you intend to make, so that you're better able to do that job well.

- Who is the decision maker?
- What is their current situation?
- What are their goals and objectives, as you understand them? And what are your goals and objectives as it relates to them?
- What potential problem areas or need areas will you need to uncover, probe, and focus on?

- What objectives should you be seeking to achieve with this account on this sales contact?

- How about on the next call or contact? And how about overall, what would you like to achieve with this client? If the key contact that you have now is not the decision maker for this, how can he or she influence the outcomes that you're trying to achieve, how can they be an asset to you even though they're not the decision maker?

- What questions can you ask—specific questions—to uncover, clarify, or amplify prospect problems, needs, or goals?

- What decision-making criteria are really important to this prospect?

- What possible benefits could this prospect be seeking?

- What services or company features do you have that provide those benefits for them?

- What kind of proof do you have? In other words, what kind of letters, testimonials, brochures, demonstrations could you use to prove to the person that they will, in fact, get what you're promising?

- How can you be of more benefit to this prospect than anyone else who has called on them?

- What possible concerns or objections might come up and how might you answer those?

- Based on your objectives for this call, what specific commitment will you ask this person to make?

- Why should they want to make that commitment? Write it down.

- By what criteria will this person judge whether or not you or your company were a satisfactory solution to their problem?

- What methods, what procedures or forms can you use to measure whether or not the actual results they got did, in fact, meet the criteria that they were judging those results by?

48

By keeping all of these questions in mind and using a sales planning guide, you can be far more effective with each account, far more effective in your overall selling. It will develop a habit of thinking, that will cause you to cover many of these areas automatically; and you won't need, in many cases, to have a written guide. But first you must start by doing the written guide several times to develop that new habit pattern, that way of thinking.

■ ■ ■

THE SECOND COMPETENCY

Target
Identify Who, How, and When to Contact

What Is a Market for You?

HERE IS THE BEST DEFINITION OF A MARKET I've ever found: *A market is a group of people who have enough in common with each other that you can establish a reputation among them.*

When you build a reputation among a group of people, then every sales call becomes easier for you. *The goal of marketing is to give you a large number of people who are willing and eager to see you.* The more you can cultivate a demand for what you do, the more you can build a reputation for yourself.

But first you've got to find out—where is my market? If it's a group of people with enough in common that you can build a reputation among them, then you've got to ask yourself, what are the links that these people have to one another?

For example, I've had people say they focus on the women's

market. Now, in many cases, that's not really a market. It's half of the earth's population, for heaven's sake. And, just because they are women doesn't mean they've got enough in common that you can build a reputation among them—unless your product appeals specifically to women and not to men. What makes a market is their communication within their own group independent of your presence.

Now, leading businesswomen, or women at the management level of business, or women within a certain age group or demographic, that's different. They do have something in common. Women in sales do have something in common. But it's not just their gender. It's their gender within a particular category that makes them different from the other people in that category.

So think of the market as a group. For example, if you're selling investments, one market would be business owners. Another market would be newlyweds. Another market would be retirees. Another market would be recent college graduates, and so forth. Think about the group of people and what they have in common. Each group has a different potential from the others. Select the group that fits your needs and then ask yourself, how do I reach them?

Markets fall into two general categories:

■ Natural markets, ones that already exist and to which you already have an entry, such as your fellow high school graduates, or neighbors; and

■ Chosen markets, groups of people with whom you have to build links in order to have those connections.

Sometimes you can tap a natural market and find great sales potential. In other instances your natural markets may not hold much promise.

You've got a natural market among your family members and friends, the people in your neighborhood or community. Maybe you've been really active in the community, and you know all the people there. Because of that, it's a group of people who have something in common. Knowing you makes it more probable that you can make sales contacts in that marketplace.

The natural market is often an excellent source of potential clients. To define it, think of your friends, your neighbors, your family members, people who know your capabilities, people who would make good potential clients for you. Consider people you've met through your spouse, your children, hobbies, church, social clubs, community activities, met online, met through past employers. What about the people you do business with today? That's part of your natural market. Any of these people might benefit from having your product or service.

So, think in terms of what is a market, where are my natural markets, and which should be my chosen markets?

A chosen market is one that you decide to go after. You see an opportunity, you gather information, establish connections, develop and cultivate that chosen market.

Choose the markets that hold the potential to take you to the top one percent and keep you there.

How to Profile a Market

When you choose a particular market to go after, develop a written profile of that market that guides you to all the aspects of it. Then you cannot merely enter the market, you can permeate it with an awareness of who you are and what you can do for them.

Here are a few elements of a good market profile.

First, list the names of *key people* within that market. Who are the players, who are the shakers and movers, who are the people that everybody knows in that group? Who are the people that mold opinion, the people that others turn to and say, "What is he or she doing?"

CASE STUDY

Federal Express

In applying its sales strategy to China, Federal Express had to choose whom to target: local Chinese companies or multinationals doing business in China. The company chose to target multinationals—a customer group its global culture and business has been traditionally designed to serve. Given the choice, Federal Express was able to pretty much transfer the U.S. business model into China, including the use of its own aircraft, building a huge network of trucks and distribution centers, and adopting U.S.-style aggressive marketing and advertising.

Had FedEx selected local Chinese firms as its targeted customer segment, winning local customers would have required a significantly greater degree of local adaptation.

Source: "FedEx to Launch Delivery Into Another 100 Mainland Cities," *South China Morning Post,* Vol. 14, no. 177, August 30, 2000

Next, do a *demographic profile* of the marketplace. What are the typical age ranges within this particular market or sub-market? What are the schools that these people went to; what are the particular configurations of their business world or their personal life? Are they mostly married, are they mostly retired, are they mostly young? Are they mostly older, are they mostly experienced, are they mostly highly educated or uneducated? Much of this information can be found on a city's or industry's website.

Next, list any associations or professional societies that this particular marketplace is connected with. What publications do they typically get; what organizations do they belong to; what are their affiliations? And, speaking of publications, what else do they read? Do they read the *Wall Street Journal*; do they read the local newspaper? Do they read small community newspapers? Do they subscribe to certain online services? Where do they get their information? And, by the way, which people who write in

Camelot Music

Camelot Music learned how to better its offerings after it switched its "Repeat Performer" system from one in which clerks stamped a customer's cardboard card after each purchase to an electronic system. The change enabled Camelot to discover one Christmas that a lot of rap CDs were bought by seniors—those over 65, that is, not those in high school. Because it was obvious that these customers were buying for their grandchildren, Camelot began a targeted campaign to them, alerting them to the hot CDs that passed parental scrutiny. The campaign worked, with sales rising 37% higher than for a control group.

It pays to measure and evaluate. You never know what you might learn.

Source: "Developmental Drive", *Delaney Report,* Vol 10. no. 2, January 1, 1999

those publications do they tend to pay the most attention to? If you can quote those people, it gives you a little bit more of an "in" with that marketplace.

Next, list *major events* that take place within that market—big conferences and key events and special unique celebrations, or milestone celebrations, or times of year, awards that are bestowed within that market.

Next, *psychographics*. Do a profile of how these people think. What do they trust? What do they fear? What are their general attitudes toward this or that, especially as it relates to your product or service? What's the general mood or general mode of thinking in this marketplace toward what you do?

Then, write down in your market profile the common fears, likes, dislikes, and even the goals that people tend to set in this marketplace. Really study this group of people. What are they concerned about? What do they like? What are they really drawn toward? What do they dislike? What are the turnoffs for this marketplace? And, what are the goals that people in this particular marketplace tend to aspire to?

Next, what are the *challenges* that key people in this marketplace tend to face? Are there challenges like shortage of manpower? Are there geographic challenges—it's hard to travel, or certain weather challenges at certain times of year, great distances to travel, limited electrical access so that it's not as easy for them to get online or to do telephone communication? Are there market shortages? Are there other limitations? The better you know what their challenges are, the better you can identify where they need solutions like the ones that you bring.

And what are the catchwords, or the phrases, the *jargon* that they tend to use in this market? In certain fields they use terminology that is unique to that marketplace. If you're dealing with people in law enforcement agencies, they have their own jargon. If you don't understand the jargon, you don't understand the people. Or, even if you do understand the people, they don't think you understand them because you don't understand how they use those words. So study the phraseology and terminology that's common to this marketplace. All of this will add to your understanding of your chosen or your targeted market. The more fully you understand each market segment, the more likely you are to sell within it.

Identifying Ideal Customers

I think everybody needs to know "who is the best customer for me?" Here's how you can generate a description of that individual.

List five of your best current customers. After you have them listed, describe as many characteristics of each one as you can. How do they do business; how do they think; where did they go to school; to what information sources do they turn; what level

---

CASE STUDY

Royal Bank of Canada

In the early 1990s executives of Toronto-based Royal Bank of Canada (RBC) realized that for retention purposes, the bank "needed to understand better how to get our arms around our best customers," says Shauneen Bruder, senior vice president of marketing and planning.

The bank segmented customers into A, B, and C levels by looking not just at dollar activity, but at the overall profitability based on all their holdings with the bank. Bruder says the segmenting ensures that the bank is strategic with customers. For example, it assigned A clients to account managers, and had RBC reps make two or more proactive contacts to those clients annually, offering them specific products in which they might be interested. The results speak volumes: Between 1995 and 1997 average profit per A client increased 268 percent, and the number of A clients increased 292 percent. Such impressive increases come from "getting the right information into the hands of your salespeople at the right time; making sure they know who the most profitable [customers are]; and regularly profiling and contacting those clients," Bruder says. It also helps the bank answer the question, "How do we best allocate scarce resources against [our best] opportunities?"

Source: "A Foundation of Trust," *Direct,* Vol. 13, no. 4, March 15, 2001

---

of financial success are they experiencing; from how many different locations are they operating?

Also note from what resource they came. Were they a referral? Did they come from a response to advertising or direct mail, or what?

Similarly, do a detailed description of the characteristics of your five worst customers. By "worst" I mean the ones that are hardest to work with, the ones who are the toughest ones to please, the ones that are generating the least profitability for you in comparison to the amount of time and energy you put into dealing with them.

When you finish doing that exercise, compare your five best customers to your five worst customers and look for the characteristics that distinguish them. Then ask yourself what prospecting methods could I employ to find more of these best customers and to avoid running across more of these worst customers?

Identify an *ideal* customer for yourself. Don't focus on the negatives, focus on the positives. What does a good customer look like? What do they sound like? Where do they go? What do they do? How much money do they have? How easy are they to access?

Identify your ideal customers and then make sure you keep your eyes peeled for them.

The Friendship Tree

How many of your friends, neighbors, and family could accurately describe what you do? It's alarming how few of them know. Even in

---

CASE STUDY

Apple Computer: "The Dark Side of Loyalty"

In 1990, Apple Computer had 3.5 million "Mac fanatics" who were incredibly loyal. Apple nurtured that loyalty and focused on delivering what they wanted. It was so focused that it did not notice that its fan base was atypical of the new users coming into the marketplace. These buyers were swelling in the Windows portion of the market.

Mac users saw themselves as a tribe apart and reveled in that isolation. When Apple bet its future on following that tribe, it cut itself off from the much larger population of computer buyers who drove the growth of IBM, Gateway, Compaq, and Dell. Today we are seeing a renewal of Apple with an entirely new strategy. They have once again identified a narrow segment of the market with the desire for ease of use, yet state of the art capabilities. Their new product line may well change the game again. Stay tuned!

our own household, sometimes they really don't understand what we do and how it helps others.

Take some time to educate this natural market. Be careful not to "try to sell them," just trade information so that both of you can understand what the other person does in this world.

To help you better define your natural market, think of friends who know your capabilities and could be potential clients. For example, list old school friends, neighbors, family friends, friends you've met through hobbies, church, social clubs, or community activities. What about friends and associates you know through past employment and people you do business with today?

Any number of these people could potentially benefit from having your product or service. This natural market is an excellent source of potential clients. Friends who know your capabilities and degree of professionalism can provide the beginning of a friendship "tree" of potential clients.

An exercise that is quite popular in the seminars I lead is the following one, developed by my friend and colleague, Steve Curtis:

> List two friends in each of the categories below. As you contact each of these potential clients, he or she may be able to add two more names to help the tree grow.

Type of Friend	List Two Names
School friends	
Neighbors	
Known through spouse	
Known through children	
Known through hobbies	
Known through church	
Known through social clubs	
Known through community activities	
People you do business with	
Others	

How to Get Referrals and Testimonials

*For God's sake, don't give up writing to me simply
because I don't write to you.*

ROBERT FROST

The quickest way to grow your business is to ask for referrals. If you don't ask, you don't get.

When prospecting, many salespeople completely forget about their current customers. *Current customers are your best source for new business.*

If you have a strong relationship with your customers, you shouldn't feel uncomfortable asking them for favors. Here are some ways to develop new business from your current customers:

Ask for referrals within their company. Sure you've asked for referrals before, but were you specific about it? Probably not. If you direct a customer's thinking internally within their company, you may come up with more prospects. For example, some companies, like a bank or a real estate company, may have more than one branch. Ask if they have a new branch opening up or if new personnel have been hired. Sometimes when expansions take place, they represent new opportunities.

Fires and floods create changes. People get married and divorced. Birth and death create opportunities and needs. Things change and new opportunities emerge.

Ask for referrals outside their company. People in business tend to know people in similar businesses. If you're specializing in a certain industry, take advantage of this small world. When you solve a problem for one customer, they may know someone with a similar problem. The key is not only to ask for the sale, but to follow up periodically and ask again and make recommendations and suggestions.

Sell more of the same. Many companies, especially small to medium-sized retailers, tend to order conservatively until a product is proven. Then they break out of their habit pattern and place larger orders. But if you see that a company has the capacity to use more of your product, encourage them to increase their orders and show them how they'll benefit. Or, if a customer is using your product but not getting the full benefit they can, recommend that they do more of the same.

Also, *sell to more of the same types of people* within the company that you're currently selling to. More of the same products, more of the same types of people outside the company—look for referrals, look for opportunities. Sometimes your best prospect is the customer himself.

Cross-sell your customers. When you see the need or ability to sell other products, present them to your customers. You've already proven that you're trustworthy, so they'll listen when you suggest they carry something else or buy something else. The same principle applies to services as it does to products. Once you've solved one of their problems, solve others.

You see this all the time in the enclosures that come with your statements from various credit card companies, banks, cable television bills, and so forth. They add the flyers that tell you about their other services. When you're contacting your clients, do similar things. Drop a hint, leave a brochure, show an example, demonstrate how you can be of further service to your customers.

Then, *cross-sell to other departments.* Make sure that you are recommending your customers to the other divisions or departments within your organization, the customers who could benefit from the services they provide as well.

Also, *take time to train the other departments in what you do* and what benefit you bring to customers so they can cross-sell back to you.

Up-serve your customers. Do more for them. By staying in touch and conducting periodic reviews of their business, you may find that their needs are expanding. This means more services are needed. The key is to see their increased need before your competitor does. And that's why you stay in touch. So up-serve your customers whenever you can.

If you want them referring names to you, give them more than they were expecting. Up-serving means increasing the size, not of the transaction, but of the *satisfaction* they feel from doing business with you. Look for ways to add a little something extra. When you focus on up-serving, they feel better served, they trust you more, they're more receptive. They will recommend other people contact you or that you contact those people. *You'll find it's easy to up-serve when you get into the habit of thinking of new ways to serve your customers at no significant extra cost to you or to them.*

Testimonial letters are a powerful form of referral you can use again and again. When a customer writes you a recommendation or a letter of praise, and they say it's OK to share it with others, you can benefit from your customer's credibility and use that testimonial without having to contact your customer anew each time you need a referral.

To prepare a file of testimonials, plan ahead now. After every successful sale, ask your customer if he or she would be willing to write a short letter summarizing the benefits they got from doing business with you. A testimonial letter should add strength to your credentials, support your claims, and prove the value of your products in the marketplace.

A common mistake is securing letters that simply speak well of the salesperson, but don't specify the value of the product. For the greatest effectiveness, a testimonial letter should support the claims you make to your prospects. It should specifically state the benefit received by the customer, and describe the need addressed when you made the sale.

Build a testimonial file. Create an entire resource of testimonials for the various things you do, and the various types of customers you've done them for. Then you have a resource to turn to any time you want to strengthen your credibility.

Ten Steps for Referral Prospecting

The more people you know, the more possibilities you create. Don't think of your sales career just in terms of your own limited energy, intellect and resources. Think of it as something that can be multiplied by all the possibilities in every person you meet, and all the people to whom they are connected.

See yourself as the center of a continuum that reaches beyond just the people you see. After all, your sales success depends on your customers. And prospecting for customers is very much like prospecting for gold. Just like an old-time prospector might pan a mountain's worth of rock, mud, and gravel to find a few valuable gold nuggets, a salesperson must mine a potential area, group of people, in terms of finding individuals or companies that are truly worth digging for. These nuggets can really be worth a lot over time through repeat and referral business. So use your database, keep records, and stay aware of who is there for you to access.

These suggestions were first developed by my good friend, Dr. Tony Alessandra, author of *The Platinum Rule*.

1. Ask for specific referrals. Narrow down the customer's focus. Ask him "Who do you know?" Then give him a specific type of person, "Who do you know who is going to be retiring soon? Who do you know who has just added on to their business? Who do you know who is seeking new employees? Who do you know who just laid off a big portion of their

business? Who do you know who was recently laid off from their business? Who do you know who has just lost a lot of weight and gotten in shape and is looking for a new wardrobe? Who do you know who has been fascinated by laser eye surgery and is ready to get rid of their glasses and have their eyes surgically improved? Who do you know?" Ask for specific referrals.

2. Gather as much information about the referral as you can in advance.

3. Ask your customer for permission to use his or her name in introducing yourself to the referral.

4. Ask your customer for help in getting an appointment with that person. Have them do the introduction.

5. Contact your referral as soon as you possibly can after getting the name.

6. Inform your customer who referred the person about the outcome of your contact with this new person. Tell them how it went, report back to them; don't keep them in the dark.

7. Build referral alliances. This can be through sources such as tip clubs or building centers of influence that can refer you to other people. Or meeting and getting to know key people within the industry or marketplace.

8. Prospect for referrals just like you prospect for sales leads—actively, intentionally, constantly.

9. Rank your referrals just like you would your customers:

   A, a hot one, a person about whom you know a lot and to whom the referrer will introduce you.

   B, a warm one, you know a little bit about the referral person and you can use the referring person's name.

   C, cold, you know nothing about the referral and you can't use the referring person's name in getting to them. That one's hardly worth going to.

10. Seek internal referrals within the companies and organizations you deal with. Have them introduce you to people in other

departments or at other locations or divisions, branches and subsidiaries. Mine the ground that you're standing on; your acres of gold are probably right beneath your feet.

Six Groups Who Must Benefit from What You Do

There are six groups of people who must benefit from what you do in order for you to get all your possibilities realized.

1. Of course, **your customer** should benefit from what you do.
2. **Your company** should benefit—this should be a win/win between customer and company.
3. **Your co-workers** should benefit from what you do—not just through more work, but through your doing it in such a way that it adds a positive input into their day.
4. **Your community** should benefit from what you do.
5. **Your colleagues** in your industry should benefit from what you do.
6. And finally, even **your competitors** should benefit from what you do. Now how on earth can I say that?

Your competitors have to reach certain levels of achievement just to stay even with you. If you keep raising the bar, if your level of excellence, your quality of service is so good that they have to get better just to stay even, then you're serving your competitors by causing them to improve, as well as your customers by serving them well.

Think of that, your customer, your company, your coworkers, your community, your colleagues, and your competitors—if any of those groups are not benefiting from what you do, then you're limiting your own possibilities.

Brainstorm three things you could do this year to be of benefit to each of these groups. Then select three from those eighteen things you just generated to take action on today. The more benefits you deliver to others, the more value you give them, and the more income you will soon receive.

The Kinds of People You Need around You

A man's true worth is measured by the people
who enter his tent.

ANCIENT ARAB PROVERB

We need different people in our life who do different things for us and for whom we can do different things—people who have a certain effect on us, who we are, and how we live our lives. Look at what your relationships do for you.

We need friends—people with whom we can communicate openly. Ralph Waldo Emerson said, "A friend is one with whom I can be sincere," and, "A friend may well be reckoned the masterpiece of nature." I like that.

We also need a lover. We need our spouse or mate, that significant other person that we can care about, nurture, and care for. We need someone who does the same for us.

We need people with whom we can celebrate our successes and accomplishments. There are times when we need somebody we can brag to without them trying to repair us. Sometimes we need the opportunity to express the pride of accomplishment. It should be done appropriately, of course, but we need people we can brag to or brag with, so we can celebrate our successes. Someone who, when we do well, will say, "Hey, good for you, I'm proud of you."

We also need people to commiserate with. When we're experiencing pain or confusion or frustration, we need someone who can hear and understand our problems, without trying to fix us or without encouraging us to dwell on the problem for too long.

We need someone who will just simply say, "Tell me how that feels." We need someone we can turn to and from whom we'll get a sympathetic ear.

We also need people who won't let us dwell there too long. In other words, someone who, if we're complaining and we're expressing pain or frustration, won't let us wallow in it too long, will encourage us to change the subject or get back on the positive path.

We also need people we can think with. People who encourage us to be more thoughtful, be more intelligent, more considerate, to look at the broader and deeper and longer-term aspects of ideas. We need people who are studying and learning and researching and bringing new ideas all the time. People who, when we are around them, tend to make us a bit more intelligent.

And we need people who inspire us. We need people in our lives who, when we're around them, make us think a little bit more of ourselves, people who lift our spirits and appeal to the nobler sides of our personalities. We also need people to work with, people who will make us roll up our sleeves, put in a full day's work, and get the job done no matter what it takes.

We need people in our lives to fill lots of different roles. We need people who will cause us to be held accountable for what we did or did not do. We need people who will challenge our thinking and not let us get by with simplistic or quick fixes when a more meaningful solution is necessary. We need people who will provide good examples, people whom we can watch doing what they do and get inspired to do what we do even better.

How do you find these people? You find them in your professional relationships, you find them in your personal life, you find them living next door, you find them down the hallway in another room in your home; you find them in you children, in your parents, in your relatives. You find them in your customers, in your community, in your church, in your professional association. Everywhere we go there are people who can bring to our lives one or two qualities that might make a big, big difference in the overall power, impact, and possibilities of our lives.

At the same time, we fill some of those roles in other people's lives. We play different roles with our children than we do with our spouse. We play different roles with our parents that we do with our managers. We play different roles with our customers than we do with those in the community. But in everyone's life there's a role that you and I play. If you know how valuable that is to you and you know what kind of role you are playing with each particular person, you can be more effective at playing that role.

Please don't get the idea that by saying, "playing a role," I mean that you're doing something artificial. The best way you can fill a role is to be genuinely yourself—not to be practicing being something you're not, but to be expressing the best part of who you actually are.

Take a look now at the people in your inner circle and see what roles they fill. You may find that some people are very good for certain needs, but not for others. Take note wherever you find a significant gap, if there's not someone on your list to think with, to celebrate with, to be playful and silly with, to be helped by or to give help to, then go shopping. Go shopping for new people to bring into your life and go shopping within existing relationships for new qualities that you can bring out.

Cultivate the quality of your connections with other people, and your life will be more effective, your career will be more successful, and this world will be a better place.

Defining and Expanding Your Inner Circle

Have you ever considered that your life is defined by your relationships? Think about it—the people you connect with and interact with, day to day, are the essence of your life experience. The vast majority of what you and I do as individuals is done in the context of relating to someone, talking with someone, work-

---

Harley Davidson

Rather than trying to export its (main) product to different customer groups, Harley Davidson concentrates sales efforts on one special target niche. It intentionally keeps its motorcycles scarce (their strategy has been to try to produce just one less motorcycle than the market will bear) to maintain its image of exclusivity but gives its customers a way of embellishing the motorcycle experience via "Harley Owners Group" (HOG) membership and accessories and clothing items that portray the biker subculture. HOG serves this fanatically loyal group by providing an insurance program, travel agency, emergency roadside assistance, two magazines, member competitions, and local chapters to 200,000 members worldwide.

Source: Katherine Lemon, Robert Rust, "What Drives Customer Equity," Marketing Management, Vol. 10, no. 1, April 2001

[And as further proof of their strategic thinking, they have now launched a new "revolution" engine and motorcycle design which broadens their market appeal to new customer groups who typically weren't interested in Harleys.   —Jim Cathcart]

---

ing with someone, doing a project that benefits someone. *Our lives are defined by our relationships.*

Well that begs a pretty big question—with whom do you currently have relationships? Take some time and make a list of all the people in your life—all of the people that you see frequently, all of the people you don't see so often but you feel a strong connection with, all of the people who play a major or a minor role in your life. List all the people in your life at this current time. Date this list so that you know that it's a description of this point in time, because our relationships evolve and change over time.

Keep a file of these relationships so that you can look back on it from time to time and see how your life has evolved as it relates to your connections with other people. We define and express ourselves through our interactions with others. If we feel a certain way about ourself, then that tends to show up in who we spend time with. Generally, the people we spend time with are people we consider to be at about the same level we are in our own lives, or slightly above it if we're optimistically building toward the future.

As we progress, we tend to expand our circle of connections. By paying attention to your relationships and the types of people in that mix of relationships, you can literally upgrade your self-perception, the way you see yourself. And in many cases, upgrade your performance as well.

Improving existing relationships, adding new relationships, or eliminating unhealthy or unproductive relationships can have a dramatic impact on your career.

At the heart of your sales career is a core group, what I call your inner circle. These are the people you live your life through as a sales professional.

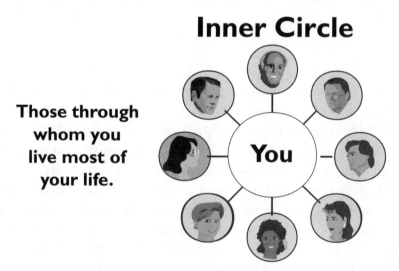

Inner Circle

Those through whom you live most of your life.

You

Take a sheet of paper, draw a circle in the center and put your name in it. Then, all around yourself, like lollipops on a stick connected to a central hub, draw circles for each of the primary players in your inner circle of business relationships: the people you know, the people you interact with, the people you work with, the people you depend on day-to-day in your sales career.

Take a look at the connection between you and each of the other people in that "socio-gram." When you look at that illustration, you see each of the individuals, with yourself in the center of them. Draw a line connecting you to each of those individuals (like the sticks of the lollipops). Each line represents your relationship with each individual.

To assess what this exercise can show you, do the following.

First, notice who is in the circle. How many people are there? Who are they? Think about each one, what talents, what skills, what points of view do they have? What do they bring to the party?

Second, notice the mix of people. What types of people are these, overall? If you looked at this as a team, what kind of team would it be? What kind of abilities do they have? What kind of attitudes do they have? What kind of special skills do they have?

Then, third, look at your connection with each of them. Look at each relationship as it stands alone and evaluate the quality of each one. By taking a look at your life from the standpoint of your primary relationships, you will have taken a snapshot of how you define and express yourself interpersonally at this particular point in your life and career.

To advance your life and to advance your career, manage your primary relationships. Add new relationships and even eliminate unproductive ones as appropriate. Take charge of your relationships and you will have taken charge of your life.

■ ■ ■

THE THIRD COMPETENCY

Connect
Establish Truthful Communication

Keeping People in the Right Frame of Mind

IN 1994 I HAD THE OPPORTUNITY TO VISIT THE WHITE HOUSE with a small group of professional speakers. At the end of the tour while our group was standing in the foyer, my wife, Paula, suddenly said, "Oh my gosh, here he comes."

We looked across the room and sure enough, there came the President of the United States. At that time it was Bill Clinton. He walked over and he spent about ten minutes with our group, one-on-one, chatting with each of us. Someone in the group mentioned that we were professional speakers and commented that President Clinton, too, was in many ways a professional speaker. Clinton looked directly at me and said, "Half of my job is keeping people in the right frame of mind."

"Half of my job is keeping people in the right frame of mind."

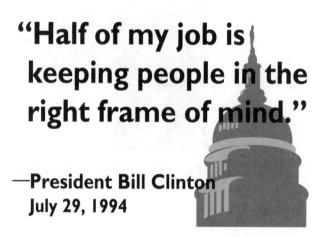

—President Bill Clinton
July 29, 1994

When you stop to think about it, isn't half of *your* job keeping people in the right frame of mind? If someone looks unfavorably at you, at what you're offering and your company, you're unlikely to get their business no matter how great your price, your product or service. But if you can keep a person looking positively at your ideas and the relationship with you and your company, then everything else will be given full consideration and you'll have the opportunity to make a sale.

Your own frame of mind has a great deal to do with your customers' frame of mind, or your prospect's. If you think your job is simply to make a sale, chances are it will show in the way you talk with your customer. But if you have a service-oriented frame of mind, if you see yourself as being responsible for finding ways to make life better for your customer through your product or service, you will produce more sales, larger sales, and a more pleasing sales experience each time.

Do you ever find yourself getting tense and uneasy in an almost desperate effort to make a sale? Any time you do that, shift your frame of mind. Shift away from making a sale to asking yourself, "How can I make life better for this client today?

How can I deal with this person in such a way that I genuinely help them?" By shifting your own frame of mind and the way you approach the subject, you can make that same shift in the way your prospect or customer views you and what you have to offer.

Managing Tension and Trust

There are two elements in a sales relationship that are absolutely vital to how that relationship unfolds: tension and trust. When tension is high between two people, the trust level is low. When tension is low, typically the trust level is high.

How do you control this? Tension arises out of the way you present yourself, among other things. So if you come on as a very strong, aggressive salesperson, a lot of times the first effect you have on other people is not bonding effect, but rather defensive. They start defending themselves from you because they see you as an aggressor.

Try this exercise: Ask someone if they would perform a simple exercise with you. Hold up your hand, and ask them to place their hand against it. Then, as they place their hand against it, start to press on their hand, pushing toward them. What you will find is they will probably push back. It's a natural, instinctive response. When we push, other people resist. They don't have to think about it, it just happens. So when we present ourselves in an aggressive mode, other people tend to resist us instead of trusting us.

In the early days of settling the western United States, settlers found that many Native Americans would greet them with an upraised hand, palm forward. This greeting was a way of showing that they were unarmed and presented no threat. When we perceive no threat, we lower our own defenses and communication flows freely.

One way that we can control tension is through the way we begin the communication, the way we present ourselves to the other person.

Tension tends to go up when you don't look trustworthy. If you don't look like a person typically would look if they were a sales professional, if you don't dress or carry yourself in the way that a sales professional would carry himself, it doesn't mean you're not a sales professional, it means you don't look like one. And if you don't look like one, people who don't know you yet won't trust you very much.

A sure-fire way that we can increase tension is by communicating in a way that's comfortable only for us. Those who are good at reducing tension, connecting with people, and relating in a positive way, tend to start by listening and observing rather than by speaking and expressing.

Present yourself to the other person in ways that make it pleasant for the other person to listen to you, to share information with you, to connect with you. As you learn to manage the tension level in the relationship, the trust level will build on its own. When we do what trustworthy people do, people tend to lower the tension level and open themselves up to more communication from us.

Think about those two elements every time you make a sales contact—tension and trust. If you want the trust, reduce the tension.

Managing Tension during the Sales Process

When tension is high, trust is low. When tension is low, trust rises.

During the sales process we go through various phases and in each phase there's sort of an ebb and flow of tension. At some points in the sales process tension is naturally always high. At other points it's naturally lower.

Tension vs. Trust

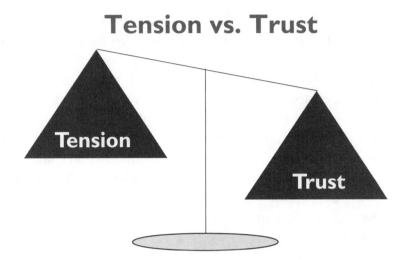

Think about the seller's tension, that's you, and then the buyer's tension, that's them. In the first phase of selling, the preparation phase, you're getting ready to do your job well. The buyer's tension is nonexistent because you're not in touch with them yet. They're out of the loop at this point. However, you are very much involved.

Therefore, your tension tends to be moderately high. It tends to go up during the preparation and targeting process, because you're working, and you're concerned about doing your job well.

The next phase is connecting. That's where you actually make contact with the person—where the goal is to generate an atmosphere of open, truthful communication. At that point, when you first make contact with somebody, their tension goes up. Your tension goes up as well. Both of you are more anxious than usual because both of you are eager to make a good connection, do the right thing, and not do something that would be harmful or unpleasant to you.

So during that process, everything you do to reduce their tension adds to the likelihood of them being open and cooperative with you.

Also, everything you did in the preparation phase helps reduce your tension in the contacting phase, because you're ready to do your job well.

As you move forward into the assessing phase, where you're studying the customer and trying to understand their needs, generally the tension drops for both you and them. Because this is simply a nonthreatening dialogue and you're asking some questions, you're empathetically listening to them, you're taking an interest in them, they're expressing only what they're comfortable expressing. As long as you don't turn it into a "third degree" (an aggressive form of questioning in which you're grilling them), then their tension stays relatively low. So you progress to the next phase.

That's when you're ready, since you understand them, to present solutions, to solve their problem. As you do this, your tension rises. But as you do this, their tension rises as well. So what do you do to bring that tension level down?

Maybe you don't want it down. Yes, you want fear and anxiety to be down, but you might want the tension level overall to be relatively above the norm in this phase of the sale. You want to generate some enthusiasm, some excitement about solving the problem. So don't be so concerned about whether there's tension present, just make sure you manage the tension so it doesn't get out of hand.

Present your ideas, show them the solutions you bring them, and then move to the next phase.

The next phase is the commitment phase, where you're trying to confirm the sale. This is what people typically call "closing," a word that I'd prefer not to use, because we want to open something rather than shut it.

The commitment phase is one in which their tension goes high and your tension goes high. Typically the salesperson is tense because they recognize that now is the time when objections typically come up, if they didn't do their job early on in understand-

"This is a safe forum for discussing your concerns. Please ignore the video recorder."

ing the person. Now is the time when sales are made or lost, if it's done inappropriately. And so the tension is up for them, the tension is up for you.

When two people are tense, the effectiveness level and the trust level are typically low. So make it a natural outgrowth of the solution process, rather than a closing experience. Just make the commitment phase the natural assumption that grows out of the previous phases. In other words, just say something that's appropriate to the setting without changing the tone between you and your prospect.

It might be something as simple as, "Let's set this up for delivery next Tuesday and we'll make this official." Or "Let me have your CPA get in touch with the research people in our department, we'll get the facts we need and we'll put this in place for you." Or "I'll send you an e-mail that confirms this and when you reply, that will give me the information I need and we can get this going." Just make it simple for them.

Then, finally, comes the assuring phase. During the assuring phase your tension tends to go way down. Hey, you made a sale—you can relax, right? No, because when you finish the sales cycle, and you walk away, their tension goes up.

That's right, they call it buyer's remorse, post-sale anxiety. Once you've departed, they're sitting there and replaying what they just did in their mind, why they did it, and trying to remember all the benefits you described. If you didn't make it easy for them to be assured that this was a good decision; if you didn't give them the facts, the tools, the information, and an orientation to that information that put their mind at ease and allowed them to easily communicate to someone else why they did it, and why it was a good idea, then they tend to experience buyer's remorse, the regret that they might have made a mistake.

That's why, even though your tendency is to relax and think about your next sale, your discipline ought to be to assure that someone is seeing to it that this new client is cared for and that their tension level drops.

Managing tension in the sales process keeps you in control of building relationships that generate profit today, as well as tomorrow.

How to Be Welcomed by Your Customers

One way to be welcomed by your customers is to be in the right frame of mind. Prepare yourself mentally for selling. What does that mean to you? What do you have to do to get into the right frame of mind to be making a sales contact?

Think about a time when you were in the perfect frame of mind for a sales call. Can you recall one? If not, just think about a time when you were in a terrific mood and really had an optimistic attitude going into any kind of an interpersonal dealing.

Take a sheet of paper and write a little narrative to yourself that describes the mood, the attitude, the situation, and the point of view that you had when that happened. Then study that and see how you can duplicate pieces of that intentionally, in the future, to keep yourself in the right frame of mind for selling.

When you can cultivate the ability to keep yourself in the right frame of mind for selling, then you go into every sales contact with confidence. You bring energy instead of drawing energy from the other person. You make a positive contribution, and people look forward to seeing you.

It is most important for you to cultivate the qualities that cause others to say, when we come through their door or over their phone line, "Here comes good news." We ought to look like an enhancement to their day, instead of a detraction from it.

Instead of going into someone's office and saying, "May I take a minute of your time (note the emphasis on "TAKE a minute of YOUR time"), we ought to go in there and say, "Do you have a minute? I've got an idea you're going to love!" The difference in those two is enormous. One of those is *taking* from them, the other one is *bringing* something to them.

Another aspect of being perceived as good news is developing a history of positive experiences with each client. Plan to make each contact intentionally upbeat and valuable to the prospect or client. If you always add something to their day, then they will look forward to your next visit.

Build the habit of finding good things wherever you go. Look for people, specific behaviors and things to compliment, bring along useful ideas, regardless of whether they relate directly to your product or not. Just be sure that they relate to your client's interests.

We should always cultivate the kind of thinking, the kind of feeling, the kind of mood, and the kind of behavior that will convey to the other person, "Here comes good news!"

Being a Partner versus a Persuader

Business should be practiced as an act of friendship,
not just a process of negotiation.

JIM CATHCART

Many years ago I worked as a bill collector. At age 22, I was working as a field representative for GMAC, collecting past due accounts and repossessing log trucks in the hills of Northern Arkansas. That's life-threatening work for anybody—repossessing log trucks in the Ozarks. I was young, inexperienced, and hadn't a clue how dangerous, potentially, this job could be.

So I went out there, boldly calling on people, at home, after dark, out in the woods with no thought as to the harm that might come to me. Happily, I never had any harm come to me, but let me tell you a quick story.

On a typical day, I would drive down some deserted logging road back in the woods. I'd find the truck I'd been looking for and I'd pull my company car up and park. I'd walk boldly over to the truck, some big hair-covered animal would step down out of the cab, he'd look down at me from about usually a head taller than I am. I'd look up, look him square in the chin and say, "I'm here to get your truck."

He'd say, "Hey boy, why don't you just leave me alone? We're alone in these woods and I don't think you want to push this issue."

And I'd say, "You know, you're right, and I am willing to leave. But you need to understand that I'm the last nice guy my company intends to send."

He'd say, "What do you mean 'last nice guy'?"

I'd say, "Well, after me they turn it over to the sheriff. People come out here with guns, and it's just not a pretty sight."

He'd say, "Now wait a minute! Before you go that far, what are my alternatives?"

I would sit down and discuss alternatives with them, and nine times out of ten I'd either get a payment, or a partial payment if they had that. Or, if they had no money at all and they were that far behind on their bills, they'd just turn the truck over to me.

Needless to say, I did OK as a bill collector. I hated the work, but I did OK. Well, the guy who came in after me didn't do so well. His name was Pete Smith, and he made a serious tactical error. He went directly from his service in the Marine Corps into bill collecting. You see, he came out of the Marine Corps with a combative attitude that he took onto his new job. It was only a few days into the job when he called on Monroe.

Monroe was a guy from whom I had been getting partial payments and late payments for about six months. Then when Pete took over, he decided it was time to clean up this account. So he goes out to Monroe's house at seven o'clock at night, in the dark, shows up on the front porch, bangs on the door, yells out some kind of a challenge. Monroe accepts the challenge, steps onto the front porch, and beats Pete Smith to a lump. I mean just absolutely beats him to a pulp. Pete's laying there on the porch, Monroe hops in the truck and disappears while Pete goes to the hospital.

Now, Pete was in the hospital for ten days over that little encounter on the front porch. I looked at that and I thought, "Good heavens, here's a guy with broken bones, gashes and bruises, who was getting hurt by calling on the same person I was calling on, for the same purpose I was calling on him. And yet that guy who beat him up was giving payments to me. What's the difference in me and Pete, other than outcome?"

The difference was attitude toward what we were doing. Pete's attitude was he was the enforcer of the contract. He was out there to persuade people to do his bidding. Do you know some salespeople who do that? They go out to persuade people to buy. Doesn't matter what the other person cares about, doesn't matter whether they've got the money or not, they're there to make the sale regardless. Well, that was Pete's attitude.

My belief was, if I tried what Pete was doing, I'd never have offspring. So I decided, instead, it would be much wiser to go out, not as a persuader, but as a partner in problem solving. I would go out each day to show the person how, by cooperating with me, they could get my company off of their back.

Be it bill collecting or traditional selling, when you go into a sales situation as a partner in problem solving, people lower their defenses and cooperate. When you go in as a persuader to talk them into buying, they raise their defenses and resist. Be a partner, not a persuader.

Which are YOU perceived to be?

Persuader or Partner?

On many occasions we intend to behave as a partner but the customer perceives us as trying simply to persuade them. In those instances it is a good idea to simply ease up and ask more questions. Listen more. Notice what the person is and is not saying.

When you become more interested in the customer, they become more interested in you. After all, in a "partnership" both parties talk and lead.

Your Unique Selling Proposition

Wal-Mart—*"We sell for less."*

Volvo—*"Safety"*

Disney—*"Magic"* & *"The Happiest Place on Earth"*

Ritz Carlton—*"Ladies and gentlemen serving ladies and gentlemen."*

A Baptist Minister—*"I sell Fire Prevention." (Think about it.)*

Have you ever heard anyone talk about having an "elevator presentation?"

The term "elevator presentation" is a quick way of describing what it is you do and why it matters to other people. This should be so short and concise that you could deliver it to another person while you were on an elevator between floors. In other words, very short, very efficient, very powerful.

Everyone needs that kind of a statement. Some people call this your competitive advantage statement. Others call it your unique selling proposition. What is it that you bring to the marketplace or to the customer that brings them value? What is it that you offer that makes their world a better place for them to be?

Try to come up with a statement that you can deliver in thirty seconds or less, which tells people your name, your company, a statement about a typical problem that people in your target market experience—and, most important, an intriguing description of how you help solve that problem.

For example, if I were in the financial services business, someone might say, "What do you do?" I could reply, "My name is Jim Cathcart, and I'm with Financial Services Company. I give people more control over their money."

85

That would intrigue most people. "What do you mean you give people control over their money?"

"Well, I mean that most people don't feel that they have the degree of control over their personal money that they would like to have. So I show them how to know what they've got, how to manage what they've got, and how to plan for having more of it so that their money is working for them, as well as them working for money."

In a statement like that you've encapsulated a lot of the value that you bring and you've told people on what area you focus.

If you're in network marketing, the business of encouraging others to become independent business owners in an enterprise with you, what you might say is, "I give people ways to take charge of their career and make their own life work even better." "What?" Describe your name and your company, but tell them that you're giving people ways to make their own life even better, while building their own business.

The ideal response to an elevator presentation or a unique selling proposition is, "What do you mean?" or, "Tell me more." If you're giving people business opportunities by going into business with you, then let them know the value of those business opportunities. Don't explain the business opportunity itself, that's next. First, describe the value.

If you're selling automobiles and someone asks you what you do, say, "I help people travel in style."

They might respond, "Oh, you're a travel agent?"

"No, not in the traditional sense. But I certainly help people make every trip a little bit more pleasant and do it in style. I represent XYZ Luxury Cars." And tell them what you do for people.

Focus on the value, for heaven's sake. That's the key here. The unique selling proposition is the value you bring, not the product or service you sell. So come up with a little, quick statement that tells people what you do.

The most unique elevator statement I ever heard was this: "I'm in the fire prevention business." As it turns out, he was a preacher. His message from the pulpit each Sunday was designed to guide people to heaven, not the other direction. So he was "selling fire prevention."

What is your unique selling proposition?

Three Essentials for a Healthy Relationship

A healthy and productive relationship requires three elements:

1. A mutual commitment to making the relationship work
2. Open and frequent communication between the participants
3. Knowing what you expect from each other

For each relationship you have, ask yourself whether these three essential elements are in place. Are both parties mutually committed to making it work? Is there open, frequent communication in which we clearly tell each other the truth? Are we clearly aware of what we expect from each other?

The quickest way to develop commitment is to work on communication. The more open and honest your communication and the more frequently you are in touch with that person, the more likely they are to feel committed to the relationship.

Clear expectations also depend on communication. First, look at your own expectations. Do you expect the other person to give you access to useful information? Do you expect him or her to call you when a problem arises, or to solve it alone via your website?

To cultivate these three essentials, choose one at a time. The more fully you show your commitment to the other person, the more you will get commitment in return. If you find that most of your relationships are one-sided in this area, then perhaps you have been reluctant to make more of a commitment. Tell yourself the truth and work on being more generous even before you have tangible justification for doing so.

To get open communication, give open communication. Practice disclosing more when appropriate. Share your own thoughts and feelings. And listen better. Good listeners generate more openness than those who are just good talkers.

For clear expectations it is valuable to occasionally review what you are looking for from each other. Review what you are trying or hoping to achieve and discuss how you can help each other to achieve it.

These three essentials will work together to make all your relationships more productive and more satisfying.

Key Telephone Skills

The telephone enables you to hold a long, relaxed conversation without being interrupted by the ringing of the telephone. Unless, of course, you have call waiting, or you drive out of cellular range, or . . . well, never mind. The phone is just another communication tool which can used or abused.

AUTHOR UNKNOWN

Here are twenty-two quick ideas on how to be better on the telephone.

1. Arrange a specific time each day to make calls. Honor that time. Keep it as an appointment with yourself.

2. Determine the number of calls you're going to make and stick to that number.

3. Establish an objective or goal for each call before picking up the telephone.

4. Fine-tune your script or outline until it's perfect for you.

5. Internalize the script so it sounds natural and you feel comfortable delivering it.

6. Develop a pleasing voice, which comes from a pleasing attitude.

"There's a bit of static on the line. Is my
sincerity and confidence coming through?"

7. Exude confidence and competence over the phone. Sit up straight. Talk with a smile on your face.

8. Match the vocal pace and the timing of your prospect.

9. Be sure you know who the decision makers are.

10. Get useful information about the decision makers from their coworkers in advance of the call.

11. Turn the decision maker's assistant into an ally. Use humor if you can. Find out their name, and use it.

12. If necessary, sell the decision maker's assistant on the value of their doing business with you. They may be the one who makes appointments for the boss.

13. Find the right times to call to increase your chances of getting through.

14. Have your notes in order before making phone calls.

15. Don't let interruptions break up your phone calling sessions. Keep your appointment with yourself.

16. Keep records. You can't improve without knowing what to improve.

17. Keep yourself motivated. Aim for at least one small success every day.

18. Make phone calls during the time of day that you're the most alert and energetic. Mornings work best for most people.

19. No matter where you are in your telephone session, follow up a success with another phone call quickly thereafter. Success breeds success.

20. Be sure to pronounce people's names correctly. When in doubt, ask them.

21. Be courteous no matter what. Ask permission to launch into your presentation, say thank you, and be sure you're not calling at a bad time.

22. Realize that any call you make is an interruption of something. Make your calls brief and keep them effective. Be a pleasant interruption.

Using Letters and Testimonials

E-mail is NOT a substitute for personal contact when dealing with major or minor customer service problems. A recent survey conducted by *Computing* magazine of 900 sales and marketing professionals discovered the most effective ways of communicating with customers when bad situations arose. The survey revealed that e-mail messages paled in comparison to making personal calls to customers and also showed that participants believe they must take personal responsibility to communicate a problem to a customer instead of passing the buck to somebody above or below them.

Do you use direct mail in promoting your business? By direct mail I mean sending letters specifically to a group of people on an ongoing basis. Not just sending out a bulk mailing, but sending out a mailing that's targeted to certain people, with a message that unfolds over time. That's how direct mail can best be handled. Think of it as a system, not an event. It's a process that continues.

In your direct mail campaign, first tell them what you do, what product or service you offer. Let them know in the first mail piece that you exist, and explain what you do for the world.

Secondly, validate what you do in your next mailing. Prove to them through an example or a testimonial, an article, or a clipping about you. Show them that you, in fact, do what your first mailing said you could do.

In the next mailing, give them a little bit more validation of your value. At the same time, tell them who else you're doing business with that they might know, which of their friends are currently using your product or service, or are involved in your organization.

Then, continue to stay in touch with new bits of information that keep expanding their awareness of your existence.

Think about how, on an ongoing basis, you could eliminate sales slumps from your year by filling in a constant outreach of messages going through direct mail. It can be done by sending a few pieces of mail a day. But make sure you always send a few pieces of mail each day. And do it in a systematic pattern, to a pre-identified group of people with whom you want to cultivate a relationship.

My friend Rick Barerra, a sales trainer and author, cultivated a four-letter-a-day system. He would send one letter a week, for four weeks, to each prospect. Send four of them a day, and then call for an appointment three to five days after sending the last letter. So send four letters a day to your target market. No more, just four. Because after a couple of weeks you'll be sending out twelve to fifteen letters a day; the first letters, the follow-up letters, the third letters, and so forth. If you're at sixteen letters a day, you're eating into your other productivity.

If you become overly enthusiastic and you contact more than four new prospects a day, you'll soon be overwhelmed when it comes time to do all the follow-up. Set up the system so that after the first piece of mail goes out, the next one comes a week later, the next one a week after that, etc. This way, over five weeks, each prospect is getting a letter a week from you. Four a day equals twenty people hearing from you each week.

In that letter, be sure that you've included the right things to build the credibility you want. For example, a customer of mine once said to me, "Jim, would you like me to send a letter to my colleagues across the country to let them know about what you've been doing for me?"

I said, "Absolutely, and pardon me for not being the first to ask."

He said, "No, I'm happy to do that. I really like what you've done for us, so I'll send out a letter." He said, "Now, if you'll just go write it, I'll mail it."

I went back and wrote a letter, telling what I had done for him, in his name. When I presented it to him for approval, he tore it up! I was hurt and asked, "Was the letter so bad you no longer want to do it?"

He replied, "No, Jim, it was too mild. You're being too humble. Tell them what you can do!" He then drafted one that truly sang my praises.

It was wonderful. He could brag about me a lot more credibly than I could brag about myself.

We decided to mail all of his colleagues at first and then to work them a few at a time. When we sent out that letter to 180 people, a lot of them responded. On the first mailing, people who'd never heard of me responded because they were finding out about me from one of their trusted and admired colleagues.

When my next letter went out, it had an enclosure of a couple of my brochures. It said, "You recently heard from my friend and customer Joe. I've enclosed the following to give you a better sense of the type of work I do and have done for him. Whenever I can be of service to you, please contact me."

Now notice, I didn't ask them to call, I just said let me know if I can be helpful. I sent them my brochures.

So the first mail they got had an announcement that I exist. The second piece of mail they got, which was a couple of weeks later, had validation or proof that I can help. And it had some brochures to tell the details.

The third letter went out after I'd already gotten the first few sales from this. It was a few weeks later, and now I had some new clients. So it said, "Dear Scott, since our last correspondence, I've worked with the following of your colleagues." Then it listed them.

Notice that "since our last correspondence" implies that you and I are friends and we've been in touch with each other. When in fact, it's really been only one way—from me to you. But I haven't stated it in such a bold, brash way that I'm taking license. I'm just implying the friendship before it really blossoms. "Since our last correspondence, I've worked with the following of your colleagues. Here's a list of their names, what I did for them, and their phone numbers. Feel free to call them if you'd like to find out more about what we could do for you."

So I've sent three pieces of mail. The first one from a client, the second one with my brochure, the third one with a list of their colleagues who have agreed to serve as referral sources, and contacting information. Next thing you know, I'm getting phone calls and e-mails from these people saying, "Tell me more."

I reached out on an ongoing basis to a specific group of people. In that case I sent a lot of letters out at first and waited for some response. But in time, I started identifying just a handful of them, like Rick Barerra's plan, and sent out four or so at a time and then built on that.

As I became more and more targeted, out of that group of 180 potential prospects that I could have worked with, thirty of them hired me for full-scale training programs. That was in a period of about three years.

Think about the implications for you. How could you use a similar strategy to get in touch with people, stay in touch with people, and over time expand their understanding of what value you can bring?

Over time, I converted from the letters to a newsletter. Once my name was established, once they understood the value I could bring, then all I needed was to give them a continuing series of messages that said, "Here's another idea, here's what Jim's done for this person, here's what Jim could do for you."

The newsletter became popular, the calls continued to come, and it will work for you as well. Think of how you could adapt that thinking to your business today. You may incorporate e-mail strategies and web links as a more efficient way to convey information, but be sure your intended audience is e-mail savvy and can access your website without difficulty. If it is awkward for them to do, it is unlikely they will do it.

Start the process now, then just stay in touch. The business will come.

Public Speaking Skills

---

*Too many public speakers begin by saying they
have nothing to say, and then take an hour
to prove it.*

WILLIAM LYON PHELPS

One very effective way to get your message out to the community, or your marketplace, is by giving presentations. I mean speeches and public presentations, not just individual sales presentations. The reason this works so well is that you're able to reach many more people. When you have a group of people gathered together and you're able to present your message, you have their undivided attention. You've got the opportunity to dramatize your message, to illustrate it with audiovisuals or a special demonstration. You have the opportunity to entertain questions and perhaps answer a question for one person that may be lingering in the mind of all the other people in the room. You can even plan questions. Have someone in the audience ask one or two questions, so you're able to talk in a more relaxed manner. There are lots of ways you can do that and the benefits are enormous.

The most persuasive form of personal communication that we have is face-to-face public address. Think about it. When a person is in the front of a meeting room, they're the only one speaking. The spotlight is on them. They've been introduced by someone else telling why they're there, and why they are a valuable resource on this subject. That's very persuasive! If they're an effective speaker, the audience will be more likely to be persuaded than they would have been in a one-to-one conversation. The credibility that goes with being the person in the front of the room giving the speech is a very effective form of communication because of the power of the position.

So here are some tips, for whenever you give a speech, that will make you more effective and make your speech more powerful:

1. *Know your audience.* Find out, Who is this group of people? What are their backgrounds? What do they expect from this presentation? Why are they here? What business positions do they occupy? What are their common needs as it relates to your subject? Know your audience. Know what they expect from you.

2. *Know your stuff.* In other words, get your material together. Know what it is you're going to talk about. Know what key points you're going to make. Make no more than three to five key points. Illustrate each one with a good story or state some

facts. Provide a demonstration or a visual to drive that point home and then summarize it.

3. *Use a catchy title.* A clever title not only describes your speech, but it piques the curiosity of the audience. It can and should make them want to attend. It puts a little playfulness into the presentation.

    Professional speaker Joel Weldon delivered a speech one time to the National Speakers Association about the importance of paying attention to the little details. His title was: "Elephants Don't Bite." He asked in the early part of his speech, "How many of you have ever been bitten by an elephant?" Of course, no hands went up. Then he asked, "How many have bitten by a mosquito?" and all the hands went up. He said, "See! That proves it. It's the little things that get you." Create a catchy title for your own presentation.

4. *Do your homework.* Research company records, the library, magazines, telephone interviews, websites, whatever is necessary to bring interesting and vital current information to your speech.

5. *Stick with your outline.* Unless you're a professional performer, have a clear outline in front of you. Feel no fear or reluctance to use your notes, and stay with your outline.

6. *Introduce the subject you're going to talk about.* Identify the key points within it. Describe, deliver, and illustrate each of those key points. Summarize what you just said. Then, offer a closing statement. It's simple—not easy, but simple.

7. *Concentrate mainly on your introduction and conclusion.* In your introduction you've got to let this audience know why they should listen to you, at this time, on this subject. What is it that makes you an authority, what is it that makes your material worthy of listening to, at this time, for this group of people?

    One of the biggest problems with amateur speakers is they don't know when to stop speaking. You'd think if they don't have their stuff together in delivering the speech, they'd end early. No, a lot of times they go on indefinitely. Maybe they're afraid to conclude too early, or afraid they'll miss a key point. But if you know exactly how you're going to conclude your speech, if you know your last statement or two, your last key point that you want to drive home which summarizes the rest of it, and you've rehearsed that in your mind, or even have it down on paper, you can deliver that whenever it's appropriate and end your speech on time.

8. *Plan a question-and-answer period at the end.* This is usually for a more relaxed forum and allows you to interact with the audience.

9. *Rehearse regularly for your speech.* Practice it aloud in front of a mirror if you need to. Do that until you're smooth and comfortable with it.

10. *Stay on time.* Regardless of what happens, stick to your time frame.

11. *Show up early. Make sure all the systems are a go.* Check out the meeting room, make sure it's set up properly. Make sure that the public address system works, that you know how the microphone on/off/volume switches work and where they are, and that you have turned on the lights or turned off the lights in the appropriate sections of the room for the illustrations or slides that you want to use. Be extra sure there is plenty of light on you the speaker.

12. *Vary your eye contact during your speech.* While you're presenting, don't just speak to one group of people; speak to the entire audience. Move around during your speech. But make sure you don't move so much that you're distracting the audience. Have a purpose to the movement.

13. *Finally, hang in there.* Your stage fright will go away in direct proportion to how well you have your act together and know your stuff. As well as how well you have your information in mind and you know your audience, and how well you've rehearsed and prepared so that you know yourself.

■ ■ ■

Assess
Understand the Person and Their Situation

Listen—and Learn

ONE OF THE VITAL PARTS OF THE SALES PROCESS IS UNDERSTANDING the person and the situation—understanding your prospect or customer. There are several things that will help you become better at understanding other people and their situations.

1. *Listening.* You've got to be able not only to hear, but convey to the other person that you genuinely want to hear.

The first meeting with a prospect is a time of discovery for me. I do more listening than talking. After they've given me one priority, I ask for a second and a third. Then I reconfirm their prioritized order. If I don't deliver my presentation addressing their priorities in order of importance, I've blown my sale.

PAT LEONARD

2. *Learning to qualify your prospects.* Know who is worth calling on. Know, once you're with someone, whether this dialogue is worth continuing or whether you ought to move on to someone else. If it's not going to end in a good sale for you and for them, maybe this isn't the place for you to be today.

3. *Determining how buying decisions of this type are made by this person or in this client's company.* You need to know how they make decisions like this: Do they check with someone else, do they do an analysis first, do they just go with their gut and say "yes" or "no." How are decisions like this made?

4. *Identifying the need gap for each customer or prospect.* What's the gap between what they have currently, and what they need or want?

5. *Confirming that customer's felt need and their strongest interest.* When I say "felt need," I mean, for example, someone might need a better financial plan, but if they don't *feel* the need for a financial plan, they're probably not going to do anything about it. So confirm what it is they feel a need for. If they feel a need for more control over their own life or career, focus on that. If they feel a need for a little more safety, a little more security, a little more reassurance, confirm that so that you're able to move forward building on what they care about.

6. *Identifying the personality pattern of your prospects and your clients.* In other words, know whether they tend to be of one behavioral type or another. Know whether their values and your values are similar. Whether their velocity and your velocity are compatible, whether their intellectual bandwidth and the way that you're presenting your information are compatible. Understand more about the personality patterns of your prospects and your clients.

7. *Asking good questions.* It's not enough to just stimulate the person to give you information that you need—you need the

"That's uncanny! How did you know that we formed the company in the early '70's?"

skill, personally, of asking good questions. What are the types of questions, what are the ways you could phrase those questions, what could you do to sharpen your skill in encouraging other people to tell you what you need to know?

When you do these seven things—sharpen your listening ability, learn to qualify prospects, determine how the buying decisions are made, identify the need gap, confirm the customer's felt need, identify their personality pattern, and learn to ask good questions, then you truly are able to understand the situation and the person.

Understanding Needs—Which Do You Address?

One of the greatest ways to be a more effective salesperson is to understand human needs. We all have needs, some of them basic, others sublime. Think of ways that you can meet some of the following customer needs through what you do in your selling. We

---

CASE STUDY

INTUIT

The company that revolutionized the way business owners manage their finances saw their greatest competitor was not in the industry. As INTUIT founder Scott Cook recalls, "The greatest competitor to small business owners was the pencil. The pencil is a really tough and resilient substitute. Yet the entire industry had overlooked it."

By simply asking potential buyers of QUICKEN software why they preferred a pencil over the computerized solutions, INTUIT learned two critical insights: the pencil was much cheaper and easier to use.

INTUIT focused on bringing out both the decisive advantages that the computer has over the pencil—speed and accuracy—and the decisive advantages that the pencil has over computers—simplicity of use and low price—and eliminated everything else. With its user-friendly screen that replicates the user's own checkbook, QUICKEN is almost as simple to use as the pencil. Further, INTUIT deleted all of the sophisticated features that were part of the industry's conventional wisdom and offered only a few basic functions most customers use. Simplifying the software cut costs. The end result was a breakthrough value created by QUICKEN and a re-creation of the industry—led by INTUIT.

Source: Harvey Kim, David Mauborgne, "Getting It Done," *Brand Strategy*, October 1998

---

have all these needs on some level. Notice these needs in your customer and you'll notice more selling opportunities.

- The need for recognition
- The need for physical comfort
- The need to be competent
- The need for timely service
- The need to avoid stress
- The need to be understood
- The need for self-esteem
- The need to be remembered
- The need to be respected
- The need to be needed and wanted
- The need to make one's own decisions
- The need for information
- The need for connections with other people
- The need to trust
- The need to be trusted
- The need for emotional support
- The need for laughter
- The need for intellectual stimulation
- The need for meaningful work
- The need for accomplishment
- The need to be successful
- The need for recreation
- The need for self-disclosure

The more you can recognize one's needs, the more you can understand the connection between what you bring, and what they need, and the more likely you are to get the sale. How many of the above needs can you meet for your next customer?

CASE STUDY

Revlon

Charles Revson, founder of Revlon cosmetics, was said to be a firm believer in the critical role people play in the marketing mix. He was often fond of saying, to seemingly anybody who would listen, "In the factory, we make cosmetics; in the store, our people sell hope."

What the Customer Experiences

There are three elements that will determine the success of your sales career: the people, the processes, and the products.

When a customer looks at you and your company, what they see is the people they deal with, you and the others who provide what they want. They see the processes they have to go through in order to deal with you. And, they see the products or services

---

CASE STUDY

Cadillac and Lincoln

In the 1990s when U.S. luxury car makers surveyed customers, they often asked such questions as "How satisfied are you with the cleanliness of our service department?" and "How comfortable was our waiting room lounge?" and other questions about less essential aspects of the customer's sales experience. Customers often responded that they were "highly satisfied." But many of those same car buyers shortly thereafter traded their Cadillacs and Lincolns in for a luxury import, such as a Lexus or Infinity. Why?

The surveys had captured the customer's satisfaction levels, but not the importance of the items being surveyed. That's like getting "A"s in courses that don't count toward your diploma. Be sure you know what your customer cares about before resting on your performance reviews.

---

that they get from doing business with you. All three of those areas can be influenced by you.

What the Customer Experiences

People   Processes   Products

As salespeople, we *are* the people in this equation. We are the ones who are providing the sales services. So we can upgrade the experience the customer has in dealing with us by focusing on the ways in which we connect with them.

The processes. What does a person have to go through in order to deal with you? Do they have to fill out a lot of forms? Do they have to look up a bunch of information to fill in those forms? Do they have to go through a series of trials and tests and other steps to get to a point where they can start receiving the benefit of your product or service? Do they have to order through some remote location or in some convoluted way that makes the buying process awkward for them?

As salespeople we can often streamline this buying process and make it much, much easier for them to get what they're seeking from us.

Our product or service itself. What the customer sees and experiences can be enhanced by us through staying in touch and monitoring their experience of using what we have sold. You see, the company doesn't know what the customer's experience is once they've bought, unless somebody tells them. That's our job. It's up to you and me to constantly feed back to the company the information that lets them know what's working, what's not working, what's popular, what's unpopular, what's easy and appealing, what's difficult and unappealing to the customer.

Our feedback of information may influence our company's plans for the next year, and for the next product line or the next product enhancement, and things constantly get better, which makes your job and mine as salespeople much, much easier.

So we have the people, the process, and the products. Those are what the customer perceives when they look at us or when they deal with our company. But overriding all three of these, what the customer experiences most of all is the feelings they get from the people, from the processes, and from the products. When we understand how to help the customer achieve the feelings he or she wants, then we will understand both how to assure customer satisfaction, and increase future sales.

Know What to Be Curious About

One of the two sustainable strategic advantages in the new global marketplace is an obsession with customers. Customers, not markets.

TOM PETERS

I think more important than knowing what to ask about is knowing what to wonder about. Until you are curious about the right things, it doesn't matter what kind of question you come up with.

The questions ought to grow out of the needed information. Here are some questions that you'll often need to answer.

- How will the customer use your product or service?
- Who else is bidding for this customer's business?
- When will this decision be made?
- What other needs does the customer have?
- How could this person benefit from having more than one of your products or services?
- How long is their payment cycle?
- Why is this particular item so important to the customer?
- Where does the decision maker go to get his or her information?
- If there's more than one decision maker, in what sequence are decisions like this one made?
- How are major decisions made within this organization?
- Who reports to whom? To know in advance, check with an assistant to determine titles and the sequence of their reporting to each other.
- Is there a break-off point where this person's decision-making authority ends? For example, does he or she need to consult a supervisor or someone else for decisions when they go above a certain dollar figure?
- Does someone else screen purchases before the buying decision is made?
- In the case of a committee, who will present your ideas to the group, and who has the most authority to make a decision on that committee?
- Who, besides the decision maker, really has an influence on the choices that are made?
- What does the buyer really want and need?

When you know what to wonder about, you'll know how to structure your questions to get the right answers. Use this as a checklist prior to each sales contact.

Tips for Effective Questioning

Here are ten tips for more effective questioning:

1. **Ask permission.** May I ask you some questions about your business? Too many times people *tell* us what they want. They don't ask, they tell. They say, "Let me ask you a question." Now notice, that's a demand, that's not a request. Instead say, "May I ask you a few questions about your business?" Or, "May I ask you a question?" It is much more courteous. Ask permission.

2. **Start broad and then get specific.** "Tell me about your business." That's a broad, non-threatening way to begin a dialogue. When you say, "Tell me exactly how much absenteeism you have in a typical week," now you're getting specific. Those could be perceived as more threatening questions. So begin with the broad questions, develop the dialogue, and then become specific as you move along, coming in finally to exactly the things that you really need to know to finalize the commitment.

3. **Build on the previous responses.** When someone says something to you, remember it and say it back to them in your future statements. For example, a person says, "I own six flower shops that specialize in decorating for large events."

   Your response, "You specialize in large events, why did you chose that niche?"

   They say, "Lower overhead, I can work out of a warehouse rather than a storefront, I don't have to maintain perishable stock, I can order in large quantities only when needed and that keeps my prices down."

You come back, "What do you specifically mean when you say large events? How would you define that, and what are the minimum size orders you deal with?" What you're doing is just incorporating a little bit of what they say in each thing your say back to them to show them that you're listening.

4. **Use the prospect's industry language or jargon when appropriate.** When you're talking to an expert, don't try to be an expert at the same level as they are, but show your own expertise or understanding of their expertise by asking questions using the right language. If you're talking to a neophyte, don't embarrass him or her with your technical jargon. This is especially true in retail sales where customers look to the salespeople for guidance. They don't want to be confused by your big language, they want to be enlightened by your understanding.

5. **Keep your questions simple.** If you want answers you can use, ask useful questions. Keep your questions to one, simple part. Don't ask two-part, three-part, four-part questions.

6. **Use a logical sequence for your questions.** People want to know where you're headed with this, where your questions are going. If they can't tell, they might feel like you're trying to manipulate them. So, ask in a logical order; start with broad, go to specific.

7. **Keep questions non-threatening.** Ask your questions in a way that is open ended and that does not touch on sensitive areas unless they absolutely have to.

8. **If a question is sensitive, explain why it's important.** It makes sense to justify a sensitive question to your prospect. After all, they have a right to know why you want to know.

9. **Focus on the desired benefits.** Not all prospects are experts in their particular field; many of them need to be informed and educated, especially about your products, features, and benefits. So ask them what they want to achieve, not necessarily how they

think they'll achieve it. That keeps you in the position of being able to show how you will fulfill those needs.

10. **Maintain a consultative attitude.** Ask questions as a consultant, and advisor, in a way that yields the most information with the least strain or tension. Ask questions in a relaxed manner and patiently wait for the responses; listen well, invest a little time now and you'll save a lot of time later.

Ten Keys to Active Listening

Here are ten keys to being a good listener:

1. **Resist distractions.** Ignore the internal noises that get in your way. When you're thinking about something else, you're not thinking about what the person is saying to you.

2. **Take notes.** People remember about twenty-five to fifty percent of what they hear, so take enough notes to help you recall the full content of the conversation—especially in a sales situation. You might want to ask the other person, "Do you mind if I take some notes?" Just write down a few notes, but don't make it awkward, make it natural.

3. **Let people tell their story.** When getting to know someone, or when listening to the customer's problem, let them tell the story they way they see it. Don't interrupt them, don't edit what they're saying, hear what they're saying, understand them. A lot of value is revealed in a person's narrative. Save your questions or comments for later.

4. **Offer verbal feedback.** Little cues that let them know you're listening: "Uh huh, yeah, oh, yes, I see, sure, I understand, OK, got it."

5. **Listen selectively.** Read between the lines, look for the important things that people convey in the way they're saying something, or maybe even in what they're not mentioning. Sometimes what they mean to say is contained more in what they left out than what they focused on.

"My ears just fell off! Hold my calls!"

6. **Relax.** Create an environment in which your customer or prospect will feel comfortable telling you what they've got to say.

7. **Listen with your entire body.** Recognize that they're not just noticing your ears and your mind, they're noticing your body. People send clues when they're not listening. Use good eye contact, but don't stare them down. Nod in agreement, relax, make it easy for someone to tell you what they have to say.

8. **Be aware of personal space.** If you get too close to someone, you create more tension. If you get too far away from them, you create more tension. Be at a comfortable distance for them.

9. **Ask questions.** Gently probe with the types of questions that expand the discussion and allow the person to share more information.

10. **Show that you care about what they're saying.** If you don't sincerely care what someone has to say to you, you're going to have a hard time being a good listener. And you can't fake it. There's no such thing as a totally uninteresting speaker. There are only uninterested listeners.

Irritating Listening Habits

Here are twenty-three irritating listening habits—things that people do or don't do that cause you or me to feel like they're not listening. Catch yourself on those that you're guilty of and learn to eliminate as many of them as possible.

1. He does all the talking. I go in with a problem, never get a chance to open my mouth.
2. She interrupts me when I talk.
3. He never looks at me when I talk, I'm not sure he's listening.
4. She continually toys with a pencil or paper while I'm talking, I wonder if she's listening.
5. His poker face keeps me guessing whether he understands or is even paying attention to me.
6. She never smiles, I'm afraid to talk to her.
7. He changes what I'm saying. He puts words in my mouth.
8. She puts me on the defensive any time I ask a question.
9. Occasionally he asks a question about what I've just told him that shows he wasn't paying attention.
10. She argues with everything I say—even before I have a chance to finish my case.
11. Everything I say reminds him of some experience he's had, or heard of. He always says, "You know, that reminds me," and he's always doing a one-upmanship. He knows or did more than I did.
12. When I'm talking, she finishes my sentences for me.
13. He acts as if he's just waiting for me to finish so he can jump in with something of his own.
14. All the time I'm talking, she's looking out the window at something else.
15. He looks at me like he's trying to stare me down.
16. She looks like she's appraising me. I begin to wonder if I have a smudge on my face or a tear in my jacket, or something.

17. He looks as if he's constantly thinking "no," or questioning the truthfulness of what I'm saying.

18. She overdoes showing she's following me—too many nods of her head, mm mm's, uh huh's.

19. He sits too close to me.

20. She frequently looks at her watch or the clock while I'm talking.

21. He is completely withdrawn and distant when I'm talking.

22. She acts as if she's doing me a favor by seeing me.

23. He acts as if he knows it all—frequently relating incidents in which he was the hero.

How many of these are you often guilty of? Are you sure? Find a truthful friend and seek input as to your listening habits.

"By the way, what's the office policy on smoking?"

Identifying Customer Needs

Here are some topics for you to study and things you will need to understand to be effective with each customer.

1. **Current situation versus desired situation.** What is their need gap—what they need now versus what they're getting now, what they hope for versus what they are receiving? If you know the need gap, you're better able to fill that gap.

2. **Psychological factors.** Try to discover if they're buying for prestige, for love, for imitation, keeping up with the Joneses, for fear, to avoid some outcome, for variety, to spice things up, or just purely practical reasons. What are the psychological factors in their decision?

3. **What's the prospect's point of view?** How does your prospect feel about this purchase? Is she afraid to spend the money? Is her reputation on the line? What are the personal risks and rewards associated with this purchase from her point of view?

4. **Key decision makers.** You've got to know who's playing. You've got to know the cast of characters and their input into the decision making. Otherwise, you may spend too much time with the wrong person. Know who's making the decision.

5. **Buying urgency.** Are they just shopping around leisurely, or getting bids, or in a hurry to make a deal? How important is it to them to make a decision right away?

6. **Buying criteria.** How are they going to judge whether what you're suggesting really meets their needs or not? What characteristics are most important to them? Are they buying quality, price, service, or the ability to customize? What is it?

7. **Political influences.** You may be bidding against your prospect's brother-in-law or mentor. Knowing this sure helps you make a better sales presentation. And it helps you form a strategy that's right for them. Know as much as possible about the internal politics, about the way things make this person look or the way things influence other outcomes.

8. **What about their bad experiences?** It's not uncommon for you to find accounts who have had bad experiences with your company or ones like yours. The ideal solution is to resolve the problem, if it's your company, or change their attitude to a positive one and then move on. But many times, without knowing about their bad experience, you get blind-sided by their fear or reluctance to say yes and you're not ready to respond to it. So probe to understand what bad experiences they might have had.

9. **Product or service demands.** If you are penetrating a new industry or a market, you need to find out as soon as possible whether your product or service will have to meet some standard of quality, some level of performance, or some type of certification. You need to know what the demands are before you go in there. What criteria are you going to have to meet in order to be in the game at all?

10. **What are the monetary constraints?** Part of qualifying a prospect is determining their buying power. But that changes over time. So keep your understanding of their buying ability current by asking the right questions. And if the situation turns sour, don't lose hope; sometimes they can borrow or take money from another department or budget to pay for your product or service. Your job is to show how moving that money would be a wise move on their part.

Roles and Buying Influences

In a decision-making process, you need to know who the players are. Many people in an organization may play a role in making a purchase. To make a sale you have to distinguish the major players from the minor ones, and make sure that you meet everyone who will influence the decision and interact with them in the appropriate way for their role within the decision-making process.

For example, one role that people play is *user*—they're the ones who will actually put their hands on the product and use it, implement it, get the value directly from it. As the name "user" implies, these are the people who will use the product, and their influence may range anywhere from insignificant to vitally important in the purchase decision. In some cases the users initiate the purchase by requesting the product. They might even be the ones who develop the product specifications or determine how your service needs to fit into their world.

Then there are *gatekeepers*. Gatekeepers control information to be reviewed by other members. These are the people who disseminate information; they also may be the person you have to go through in order to get an appointment with someone else. A purchasing agent might be the gatekeeper. Or they might be the one who does the screening and the detail checking. So get to know who the gatekeepers are.

Next are *influencers*. These are not users, they're not buyers, they're not deciders, they're not gatekeepers. These are people who have an impact on the decision maker, people to whom the decision maker defers for their opinion. They have important relationships with those who make the decision because they filter information in a way or they color information in a way that exerts influence on the decision-making outcome. They shape opinions, which may or may not aid the selling process.

Then you have *deciders*. These are the ones who actually make the buying decisions. Whether or not they have the formal authority to do so, the decider is the one who, in fact, makes that choice. To identify the decider is sometimes difficult to do, but it's vitally important for you. It might be the president of the firm; but then again, it might be that the president makes the final decision only after the decider gives a go or no-go.

Then there's the *buyer*. The buyer has the formal authority to make the buying commitment. This is the person who has the position, the power, the clout, the credentials, to sign the contract, shake your hand, write you a check, and get the job done. The buyer is often assumed to be the purchasing agent, but that's not necessarily the case. Many times purchasing agents just perform a clerical function. Other times they are the ones who makes the decision.

So, what if this doesn't apply to you, what if you don't deal with purchasing agents, what if you're selling to families or individuals?

Well, you still have gatekeepers that determine how information gets from you to them, or how an appointment is set, or whether it's set. You have influencers, people they respect and admire, people whose testimonial or personal example you could use to illustrate your point or strengthen your case.

The buyer and the decider may be the same person or it may be a husband and wife. It may be that one of them is the buyer, the other one's the decider. And certainly in the case of just a couple of people like that, they are the users. So you will need to cover all the bases with the one person, or two people, that you might have been covering with a full cast of characters.

Know the roles, know the players, know the functions. It keeps you in control of the selling process.

Reading People

My friend, Dr. Tony Alessandra, author of *The Platinum Rule*, says that we should practice the Platinum Rule: "Do unto others as they would like to be done unto." It's a play on the Golden Rule, treat other people the way they would like to be treated. Many years ago, Tony and I worked together as partners in the creation of a program called "Relationship Strategies." "Relationship Strategies" was based on understanding different types of people, and relating to them using different strategies, based on what kind of person they were.

There are two dimensions to this.

One is openness. With any person you meet, it's pretty easy to determine whether they're being open or not. Someone who is

---

CASE STUDY

Speaking in Tongues

Books are filled with examples of what can go wrong when U.S. businesses attempt to sell their products abroad with less than an adequate grasp of the local language and culture. When General Motors described its "Body by Fisher" in Flemish, it came out "Corpse by Fisher," which did not increase sales. Pepsi-Cola's highly successful slogan "Come Alive With Pepsi" almost appeared in the Chinese version of the Reader's Digest as "Pepsi brings your ancestors back from the grave." A U.S. airline operating out of Brazil tried to lure business people by claiming it had plush "rendezvous lounges" in its first-class sections—without realizing that in Portuguese, the word "rendezvous" implies a room for making love. Frank Perdue of Perdue Chicken fame decided to translate one of his very successful advertising campaigns into Spanish with some unfortunate results. The slogan "It takes a tough man to make a tender chicken" was translated into Spanish as "It takes a virile man to make a chicken affectionate."

As amusing as these may seem, such translation errors have cost U.S. companies millions of dollars in losses, not to mention the damage done to their credibility and reputations.

Source: John Caslione and Andrew Thomas, *Global Manifest Destiny* (Dearborn, 2001), Chicago, pp. 55–56

---

not open we call "guarded." They tend to keep things close to the vest, not show their feelings. They're more thinking-oriented. They tend to be a little bit more fact-focused, more formal and proper. People who are guarded tend not to share information readily.

The other end of the scale is someone who is open, is relaxed and warm. They're supportive, they're flexible about time, they tend to focus on the relationship before the task, they tend to share their feelings freely, they tend to be a little bit more sensitive, or at least show their sensitivity a bit more.

So the first thing to notice with each person is their level of openness. With open people *you* can be more open. With guarded people your openness might be seen as irritating, awkward, or inappropriate. Learn to recognize and understand the other person's level of openness.

Second is their directness, whether they tend to get directly to the point or take their time getting there. That goes from indirect to direct. It's a matter of pace.

The indirect person tends to be a slow decision maker, kind of passive in their behavior; they're easygoing, they tend to listen well, but they're more reserved and shy, they keep their *opinions* to themselves even though they may be showing their *feelings* sometimes. The indirect person tends to avoid risk.

On the other hand, a direct person is outgoing, they speak up, they get to the point, they take risks, they make swift decisions, they're aggressive, impatient, sometimes talkative, and you know where you stand with them.

When you combine their openness with their directness, you get four modes of behavior—what we call Behavioral Styles.

Relationship Strategies

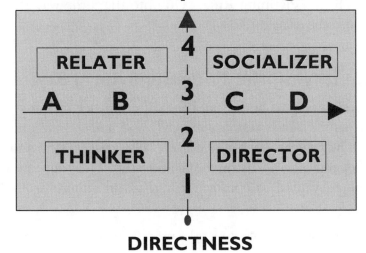

Someone who's open and direct I call the *socializer*. The socializer is the outgoing individual who will tell you what they're thinking at any given moment. You can read them like a book.

The open person who's indirect, slower paced, we call the *relater*. The relater is someone who's a people person, a team player, more soft and easygoing about things.

The indirect person who is guarded is what I call the *thinker*. The thinker is someone who is more task-oriented. They're someone who will analyze and take time to study the details before making a decision.

The guarded person who is direct is a fast-paced person that we call the *director*. The director is a person who gets right to the point. They want something done, they want it done right and they want it done now. They are very assertive people.

So there are four modes—the director, the socializer, the relater, and the thinker—four types of people. When you learn to recognize these four types—you'll be more effective in selling, because each type requires a different approach to reduce the tension with them and increase the cooperation to generate more sales.

Notice the kind of person you're dealing with so you can practice Tony's Platinum Rule: "Do unto them the way they would want to be done unto."

Identifying the Four Behavioral Styles*

Here's a way to understand the different behavioral styles—*the relater, the thinker, the director, and the socializer*—even more fully.

The *relater* is open and indirect. Their pace is slow and relaxed. They put the priority on the relationship. Their appearance is casual, they tend to conform and dress like those around them.

---

*For more information on this model and to take the free online assessment, go to *http://www.cathcart.com*

Their workplace is personal, relaxed, friendly. They get their security from friendship and cooperation, they rely on other people. One of the things they fear is sudden, abrupt change. They measure their personal worth by their compatibility with others and the depth of their relationships. They're internally motivated by involvement—they have a need to be needed by others. Their strengths are listening, teamwork, and follow through. Their weaknesses are that they are a little overly sensitive; sometimes slow to start, they tend not to set very big goals. They are irritated by insensitivity and impatience and under stress will become submissive or maybe indecisive. When they make decisions they make the decisions with other people, typically, and what they're seeking from you is a sense of acceptance and a sense that you and they will be working together. That's the relater.

The *thinker* is guarded and indirect. They are slow and systematic, their priority is on the task, their focus is on the process, and their appearance is a little more formal or a little more reserved. Their workplace will be structured, functional. Their source of security is preparation and thoroughness. They fear criticism of their work, they fear embarrassment. They measure their personal worth by precision and accuracy. Their internal motivation is the process; they love following a detailed process and they believe in personal competence. Their strengths? Planning and organization. Their weaknesses tend to be perfectionism, a bit hypercritical, slow to make decisions. Under stress they tend to withdraw or become very headstrong about the facts and figures that they're working on. Their decisions are very thorough, well thought out. And they're seeking from you accuracy and information, something they can rely on. They want to know that they can not only rely on you, but rely on your research, rely on your data, rely on your claims, rely on the warranty that comes with whatever you're offering them. That's the thinker.

The *director* is someone who is guarded but direct. They're fast and decisive, they focus on the task, they want to get results.

They're businesslike and powerful. Their workplace is busy, efficient, and structured. They tend to exert control and leadership in order to gain security, they feel most secure when they're in charge. What they fear is being taken advantage of, wasting time; they measure their personal worth by the results they get, the track record they've built, and the progress they're making. Their internal motivation is winning, being in charge. Strengths? Delegating, leadership, inspiring others. Weaknesses? Impatient, insensitive, they dislike details. They're irritated by inefficiency and indecision. It drives them nuts. Under stress they get highly critical and become dictatorial. Their decisions are decisive and quick and they seek from you bottom-line results. They want to see some productivity, they want an outcome, so they'd like for you to show them that you're going to make things happen. That's the director.

Finally, there's the *socializer*. Now here's someone who's open, and at the same time very direct. They're fast, they're spontaneous, they put the focus on the interaction and the relationship with other people. Their appearance is more bold and stylish, their workplace is personal, tends to be a little cluttered, sometimes stimulating. Source of security? Flexibility and playfulness, gaining the approval of other people. What they fear is loss of prestige or boredom. They measure their personal worth by recognition they've achieved, status, the number of friends, the kind of attention they're drawing to themselves. Their internal motivator is being included, being part of the team, being involved. And they love the chase, not just catching what they're going after, but the chase itself is fun for them. They're strong at persuading, they're enthusiastic, they're entertaining. Their weaknesses are that they tend to be not particularly good at time discipline, tend to ignore details, and sometimes appear restless. Two of the things that irritate them are routines and perfectionism. They tend to become sarcastic under stress and sometimes they come across as being superficial. They make their decisions quickly, spontaneously. What they seek is quick outcomes. They want recognition, they want to have fun, they want things to happen, but they want to be involved in what's happening. That's the socializer.

When you learn to understand and recognize the relater, the thinker, the director, and the socializer, you'll recognize which type is strongest in you, you'll notice which type is strongest in the other person, and you'll know more about how to make more sales.

How to Be Flexible with Each Style

Here are some prescriptions for flexibility with the four major personality types—*the relater, the thinker, the director,* and *the socializer.*

With the *relater*, they need to know how what you're suggesting will affect their personal situation. Do what you do with warmth, save them conflict. Facilitate their decision making by giving them personal service and assurances, guarantees. They want you to be pleasant, be supportive of their feelings and their concerns. Create a personal environment for the dialogue. Go at a slow and relaxed pace. Make sure that your priority is on the relationship with them and the communication. When you're at play, be casual and cooperative with them. Use your time with the relater to develop the relationship. In writing to them, write warmly and be friendly. On the phone be warm and pleasant. That's the relater.

For the *thinker*, they need to know how they can justify what you're talking about logically. They want to be able to explain it, they want to know how it works. So do what you do with accuracy, save them from being embarrassed. Help them with data and documentation to make a decision. They want you to be precise and to support their process, their thought process and their business procedures. Create a serious, thoughtful environment.

Maintain a slow and systematic pace and put the priority on the task and following the process. At play with them, be structured and play by the rules. Use your time with a thinker to ensure accuracy. Write to them in a detailed and precise way; spelling counts, so does format. And on the telephone be businesslike, precise, and efficient. That's the thinker.

The *director* wants to know what your product or service does, by when, and what it costs. In other words, get to the point, give them the bottom line. Do what you do with conviction, stand up for yourself, stand up for what you do, stand behind your product, save them time and effort. Help them make decisions by giving them options with supporting documentation or analysis. But don't go into all the documentation, just have it there. They want you to get to the point, support the goals they're trying to achieve, and create a businesslike atmosphere for the dialogue. Keep to a fast and decisive pace. The priority ought to be on the results, the task at hand. At play, the director is going to be competitive and aggressive, so expect that and respond to it. Use your time with a director to act efficiently. Your writing should be short and to the point; on the phone, it should also be short and to the point. That's the *director*.

For the socializer, what they want to know is how's this going to work for them, how's it going to make them look, how's it going to help them get the results they want to get, how's it going to save them time, how's it going to make life more fun? Do what you do with a socializer with a little bit of flair, a little creativity. Save them effort. To facilitate their decision, give them testimonials and incentives—testimonials from people they admire and respect and incentives they will personally enjoy or from which they will benefit. They want you to be stimulating, so support their ideas, what they care about, what they're interested in. Create an enthusiastic atmosphere, be fast and spontaneous. The priority for them is the relationship and the interaction, so put the focus on the dialogue, get them involved.

If they're not talking, they're not listening either. They need to talk, let them. At play, with a socializer, they're going to be spontaneous and playful, so you should be the same. Use your time with them, in business or not, to enjoy the interaction. When you write to them, be informal and a little dramatic. On the phone, be conversational, flexible, and playful. That's the socializer.

Those are four prescriptions for flexibility with each of the four dominant behavioral styles. If you understand those and practice those strategies, you will in fact, cultivate relationships.

Understanding Personal Velocity Differences

Every person has a *personal velocity*. It's the natural pace or intensity with which they live. Some people naturally operate at a highly intense pace, others at a slower pace.

Our modern society tends to reward the people with the higher velocity. Sales contests, sporting events, games, all acknowledge those who give it an all-out effort. But each velocity is valid—low, moderate, and high. Plenty of people who operate at a slower pace make large contributions to the advancement of business or society.

Velocity is a combination of two things—your energy and your drive. Each of us has a natural range of energy that is enhanced or limited by our nutrition, our fitness level, the amount of rest that we get, the way we manage stress, and the attitude we carry into each day. This determines the amount of that energy that's available to us that day.

Also our drive. We have a natural degree of drive or self-motivation, which is affected by things like our self-esteem, our clarity of purpose, the goals that we've set, our awareness of the possibilities available to us, and the appeal of each of the goals that we've set.

So energy and drive are both manageable within a certain range, and both of them combine naturally to determine your velocity. So what's your velocity? High? Moderate? Low? Let me describe each one.

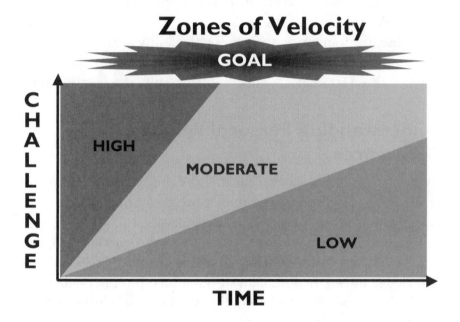

High velocity—those who are genuinely self-motivated, who love to work toward goals. They prefer long hours, they like those hours filled with a variety of activity. They use even their leisure time to advance toward their goals. They set challenging goals for themselves, big ones; they have high aspirations, they hold themselves to high standards, they enjoy competition, they find inactivity frustrating. And they expect a lot from themselves.

Moderate velocity—people who are somewhat self-motivated. They balance their work and their leisure pretty well. They prefer a standard work day with a moderate mix of activities. They use leisure time to complete chores and socialize, they also actually use it for leisure. They set goals that are generally reachable, not highly challenging, and they have moderate aspirations. They accept competition, but they don't thrive on it. They sometimes find inactivity relaxing. They have rather mild expectations of themselves. That's moderate velocity.

- **Low velocity**—those who are motivated primarily by others, or by needs, rather than inner desires. They sometimes find work demotivating. They prefer to work as a team player rather than as a leader. They don't want to be the one who has to initiate things. The use their leisure time to pursue personal or non-business interests. They pursue these interests casually, they tend to take things as they come, they seldom really set firm goals that they're going to go after. Their aspirations are rather mild, they don't like competition, which makes them uncomfortable. They even enjoy occasional inactivity, they like quiet time, and they don't expect a great deal from themselves.

Now, with those three definitions, it's real clear our society pays more money and gives more awards to the higher-velocity people. But our society is structured in such a way that there are thousands upon thousands of different jobs and roles and levels of responsibility within those jobs. Many of those call for lower velocity. Many of those are not positions of leadership, of initiative, of competition. So there's a place in our society for lower velocity, moderate velocity, and higher velocity. And, there's a place in just about every role, every sales position, every company, for lower, moderate, and higher velocity. It's all a matter of what kind of standards you're going to be measured by, what kind of goals you're trying to achieve, what kind of marketplace you're dealing with, and what your intent is.

So what is your velocity? High? Moderate? Or Low? Don't look around to see who's watching, just answer in your own mind, what do you think? Understand what your velocity is, and I'm not talking about situational velocity, I mean lifelong velocity. What is your general range of energy and drive? Is it high most of the time, moderate most of the time, lower most of the time?

When you understand your velocity, and you embrace it and say, "That's OK," instead of listening to society saying, "Oh, no, no, everybody must aspire to high velocity," once you accept your natural velocity, you're more at peace with yourself. You're going to be more effective in managing your own velocity, instead of trying to change it to a level that's more naturally suited to someone else.

Now, question number two becomes, what's your prospect's velocity? Hmm. When you go into a sales situation and you bring, let's say, high velocity, and you're calling on someone with low velocity, your approach is going to be much too intense for them, you will overwhelm them. So you need to learn to slow down and match your pace to their pace, match your drive and your ambition level to theirs. Be slightly above where they are, if you need to be, to inspire them, but not so much above that it intimidates them.

Now, if your style is lower velocity and theirs is higher, then when you call on them, you need to stretch the envelope a little bit, you need to reach a little higher, increase your expectation, let them take the initiative, let them drive the size of the discussion or the sales challenge that's in front of you.

And with moderate velocity, of course, it's just a mediation between the two extremes. Learn to recognize velocity when you see it. Learn to recognize it in yourself first. Know yourself, then you can know others. The better you know yourself, the better you know others, the more sales you make.

The Seven Natural Values

Every person has seven natural values:

- Sensuality
- Empathy
- Wealth
- Power
- Aesthetics
- Commitment
- Knowledge

Values are the relative importance of something. These are things they care about that are just part of being human. Every person cares about these seven things throughout their entire life. But each person's priorities tend to differ from the next person's priorities. Sometimes they're the same, but more often than not, there are differences between us.

When you understand these seven values and know how to identify when someone's expressing one of these values, you'll know how to sell to them more effectively. Practice the Platinum Rule—"Do unto others the way they want to be done unto." Here are the seven natural values:

1. **Sensuality**—the relative importance of your physical experience. The sensuality value relates to how important your physical experiences are to you. Everyone cares about their physical experience, but for some people it's a really high value, for others it's kind of low. Someone who has a high sensuality value shows an interest in physical experience like taste, touch, smell, comfort, fit, feelings, humidity, light, and so forth. They have a sensitivity to the physical aspects of an experience and that stands out for them. They'll say, "Let's not go to that theatre, their seats are uncomfortable and their soft drinks are watery." Even though the purpose of going to

a theatre is not the seats or the soft drink, still that's part of the physical experience for them and they would tend to notice that more than someone with a low sensuality value. With someone like that, hands-on experience of your product or service is a key element in the sales process.

2. **Aesthetics**—the relative importance of beauty, balance, symmetry, and blend. People who find this important love organized systems, they love beautiful sunsets, certain color combinations, they like paintings, landscapes, architecture, and patterns; these things appeal strongly to them. So the look of your proposal or your product may carry as much impact for them as the content of it or the use of it. They say, "That meeting would have been a lot more productive if it weren't in such a dull-looking meeting room." Hmm, aesthetic value.

3. **Empathy**—the relative importance of feeling connected to other people. People who value empathy need to be around others. They need to be around others they care about. Their helping impulse is very strong, they're drawn to the needs of other people and sensitive to their reactions and experiences. They might say, "I bought from her because I felt she really cared about my needs." With someone with a high empathy value, it really is a relationship buy. Because they buy based on how they feel about the person and the organization that they're connecting to by making a purchase.

4. **Wealth**—the relative importance of ownership and value, tangible value, monetary value. Quality for them is a major consideration. One cashmere jacket would be preferred over two wool-blend jackets, just because of the wealth value, the effect of it. The sincerity of one's words is evaluated by what they do with their money. They say, "Put your money where your mouth is and then I'll see if you're telling the truth."

5. **Power**—the relative importance of control and receiving recognition, acknowledgement, praise, special privileges, honors, titles, and prestigious things are prime considerations for the person with a high power value. They like position,

they like control, they love the idea of having their own VIP parking space or getting backstage passes, or sitting in the executive section at a meeting. They say, "This person's management idea sounded good, but he's not a manager. What could he know?" In other words, they're evaluating this person's ideas by the position he holds, which may or may not be a valid way of evaluating it.

6. **Commitment**— the relative importance of having a cause, of doing the right thing. Someone with a high commitment value puts beliefs and affiliations ahead of everything else. They want to do something that matters, that makes a difference in the world. They're on a campaign, they're on a crusade, they want to do things that matter according to the values that they have. They do what they think is right and they like being part of an organization or group that they can believe in. They'll say, "I trusted him because he walks his talk. If this guy says it, you can take it to the bank." They put a lot of stock in personal conviction.

7. **Knowledge**—the relative importance of learning, discovering and understanding. This person loves to learn. Knowledge is seen as an end in itself. You give them a book, send them to a seminar, participate in a discussion, allow them to find a way to do some problem solving, that's a gift to them, they love this. They might tend to listen to learning tapes, or public radio, or go online and do a great deal of research rather than listen to music stations or other forms of entertainment. They seem to have an endless curiosity. They say, "I feel like I've really grown, and yet I'm amazed at how little I know on this subject." Or, as my friend Jim Newman once said, "So many books, so little time."

So there are seven basic natural values that every person possesses—sensuality, empathy, wealth (think of the acronym S-E-W, sew). Power, aesthetics, commitment, knowledge. P-A-C-K, pack. If you put those two together—SEW PACK—

it's a memory tool. "Sew Pack"—think of the little sewing kits that sometimes they'll have for you in a hotel room, a little pocket sewing kit, a sew pack.

Every person has all seven values. The key to their hot buttons is found in their top values. Learn to listen for values.

How Are You Smart?

How are you smart? Notice I didn't ask you how smart you are, I asked you how you are smart. Our society, for many years, has been fascinated by how smart people are. We've developed things like the intelligence quotient, the IQ test, to measure how smart somebody is. It typically produces an implied contest; the one with the highest IQ wins.

Well, I think it's far more useful to know how someone is smart. Did you ever see the movie *Rain Man* with Dustin Hoffman and Tom Cruise? In that movie, Dustin Hoffman's character, Raymond, was an autistic savant. In other words, he was a genius and an idiot simultaneously. I mean literally, he was both at the same time. He was, in the sense of the idiocy, unable to live effectively day to day just by doing the things he needed to do to take care of himself. He couldn't carry on a normal conversation with people, he couldn't manage his own world very effectively.

However, simultaneously with that low ability, he had a phenomenal ability mathematically. He was a genius. Someone spilled a box of toothpicks, he glanced at it on the floor and instantly counted exactly how many toothpicks were there, accurately. He could look through the phone book, memorize the names, addresses, and phone numbers of everybody in the entire phone book and respond to you by giving you exactly what the person's name, address and phone number were, the minute you asked him. "What's the fifth person on the page listed under G?" And he knew. Amazing, amazing ability.

Raymond was dysfunctional. Raymond was a special case. But most everybody has certain smarts that are dominant over their other smarts.

It's helpful if you think of smarts as being different types. Not just intelligence overall, not just verbal or mathematical intelligence, but also introspective intelligence—understanding your own feelings, your own thoughts, concepts, and philosophies, knowing yourself.

Interpersonal intelligence, people smarts, knowing other people and how to respond to them, how to stimulate a conversation, how to mediate arguments, how to connect with someone else, how to be sensitive to what's going on with them, knowing the right thing to say.

Mathematical and logical intelligence, knowing how to put things in order, how to calculate, how to find patterns and relationships between things, good at analysis.

Musical intelligence, some people are very good with music. You remember tunes and lyrics easily. You use music as a frame of reference or filing system. You think of things in relation to a tune or a song. You have a natural sense of timing or rhythm, you enjoy all types of sounds. You find yourself easily distracted by sounds, you notice the cadence of things.

Physical intelligence, you learn best by doing something hands on, you want to get personal, physical contact with the subject, you feel a need to move while you're learning; your favorite pastimes probably involve activities or handiwork, you have an ability to manipulate things with your hands or to dance or move in such a way that you can achieve things physically that others find more difficult.

Visual intelligence, picture smarts, being able to use charts and symbols and visual images in your mind to make a point, to see things clearly in your mind. Being able to turn something around, take it apart, and put it back together in your head effectively.

Verbal intelligence, good at articulating, good at explaining things by choosing the right words. Using words to create pictures, using puns, creative phrasing, creating new words, enjoying expanding the vocabulary, enjoying writing and reading, putting importance on things that are verbal or written.

There are seven different kinds of smart:

- Verbal (Word)
- Visual (Picture)
- Physical (Body)
- Musical (Music)
- Math/Logical (Logic)
- Introspective (Self)
- Interpersonal (People)

This comes out of the work of Howard Gardener, at Harvard, and Thomas Armstrong, one of his colleagues, who wrote a book called *Seven Kinds of Smart*. Gardener's first book on this subject was *Frames of Mind*. Another researcher on this subject is Robert Sternberg of Yale, who wrote a book called *The Triarchic Mind*. So there's a lot of work backing this up. There are many different types of smart.

There's "word smart," that's verbal; there's "picture smart," that's visual, there's "body smart," that's physical; there's "music smart," there's mathematical or "logic smart"; there's "self smart," that's introspective; and there's "people smart," that's interpersonal. There may be many, many others.

If you recognize how you are smart, then you'll recognize why certain ways of selling are easier for you, and other ways are more awkward. What's important is not only to know yourself, but to know your customer and notice how he or she is smart.

The way you're smart is the way you're most effective in expressing something. But it might be that the way they're smart is not compatible with the way you're smart. Don't just rely on your natural strengths. Develop resources, tools, connections, illustrations, video recordings, whatever you need, some kind of a resource that helps you communicate with people whose smarts are different from your own.

Intellectual Bandwidth

Have you ever heard of the concept of bandwidth? Bandwidth is a term that's used when referring to telephone services. They talk about a particular type of telephone line, whether it's a fiber optic cable, or whether it's coaxial cable, as having a certain bandwidth. A bandwidth indicates the amount of information that can be processed at a given time, efficiently.

For example, the "plain old telephone service," POTS, they call it. POTS can accommodate a few conversations on one copper wire, at one time, but there's a limit to how much it can handle. If you change that to another type of cable, you increase the bandwidth and it can handle lots more information at one time. If you go to fiber optic, you can expand greatly the bandwidth and increase the number of communications that can efficiently go over that cable at that time.

People have bandwidth. Some people have what I call *operational bandwidth*. Their intellectual capacity may be potentially able to handle all the information in the world, but not all at once. Someone with *operational bandwidth* can handle a few ideas at a time, efficiently. However, if you start presenting several different ideas at once, they get confused and frustrated.

The next level, which I call *strategic bandwidth*, can handle more information, but still there's an upper limit to how much they can handle.

Next, the highest level, for our purposes, is *conceptual bandwidth*. *Conceptual bandwidth* would be about two percent of the population. These are people who have an enormous capacity for processing different ideas at the same time and doing so efficiently. These are people who can juggle a lot of different tasks at once, keep all the plates spinning on the poles, as they say, and keep these ideas, really, clearly in mind. They can shift from one to the other without any real confusion.

Strategic represents about eighteen percent of the population. When they look at something, they look at it not in terms of the overall concepts, they look at it strategically and they think, "How can this be used, what are some other options or alternatives?" Typically these are the people who are drawn towards sales, management or leadership positions. Not always, but typically.

Operational is about eighty percent of the population. The vast majority of people have *operational bandwidth*. That means that they're intelligent enough to do all that they need to do in their life, but that their intellectual capacity, at a certain point, gets overloaded and they get confused or frustrated beyond that. With them, the best way to operate is one or two ideas at a time, keep focused on those, get closure on those and go to the next. An *operational bandwidth* person would look at function first.

Here's an example. Let's say you take a ballpoint pen, a gold ballpoint pen. You hand it to the person and you say, "What is this, tell me about this." The operational person would say to you, "It's a ball-point pen." You'd say, "Tell me more." "Well, it's a gold ballpoint pen. What else?" "What do you want to know?" "How could it be used?" "It could be used for writing, for marking, illustrating." "Any other uses?" "Of course." In other words, it would all ultimately occur to them, but they won't just instantly start thinking of all these possibilities. They see the function and that's where they stop. Unless prompted to go beyond it. Again, that's about eighty percent of the people we deal with.

When you're presenting a sales idea, present it simply, clearly, and focus on that idea. Let them understand that one.

Think of ideas like a pearl. The idea is the pearl and you're dropping it into a bottle of thick shampoo. Let the pearl sink to the bottom of the shampoo before you put another idea in the top. With operational people, it's one idea at a time, clear focus, get closure, then the next.

Strategic thinkers—they look at that pen that you had presented to them and they say, "This is a writing instrument, but it's more than that." You say, "What do you mean?" "It could also be used to scratch your ear, it could be used to prop open a window, it could be used as business jewelry, you can put it in your pocket or purse or portfolio and it would go along with the other things you had that were similar in design." There are a lot of uses apparent to the strategic thinker. With strategic thinkers, present your idea, but explore some of the options. Think with them about the possibilities that are represented there.

Next you go to a conceptual thinker and you hand them the pen, "What is this?" They'll look at you, they'll get a little reflective, as they look off in the distance and they say, "What you have here is a symbol of mankind's ability to transcend space and time." "Excuse me?" "Yes, this pen represents mankind's ability to create a tool, created by mankind, for its own use. And it allows us to make markings which have similar meaning to different people. It allows us to make markings and draw images, which over time can communicate with people who haven't even been born yet." And you say, "Wait a minute, I really didn't want to know quite that much." Recognize that about two percent of the people you call on are going to be conceptual thinkers. They're going to be racing way ahead of where you are in presenting your information. Allow them to explore a bit, sell them on the main concept or idea, get agreement on that, on why you should talk about this business opportunity, why you should consider this form of investment, why you should consider this product versus another. Sell the why, explore the how, then commit to the immediate application, the sale that's at hand. Why first, how second, commitment third.

With the operational person, the first focus is not on the why, it's on the how. The strategic person can vacillate between the two. Just learn to recognize whether the person you're talking with is more conceptual, more strategic, or more operational. When you do, you don't have to be a scientist at this, all you've got to be is better at noticing which kind of bandwidth you're dealing with. That will help you adapt your selling to their buying.*

---

*Velocity, Values, Smarts, and Bandwidth are covered in more depth in my book *The Acorn Principle*.

■ ■ ■

THE FIFTH COMPETENCY

Solve
Let Them Experience the Value

Show How You Bring Value

A KEY AREA OF COMPETENCE AND SKILL THAT WE ALL NEED TO MASTER is solving your clients' and prospects' problems with your product or service—in other words, learning to propose solutions to them in such a way that they are compelled to act on those solutions.

One vital aspect of this is your *ability* (and your *confidence)* to give sales presentations. How's your opening—does it draw people in? How are the key points that you make, do they really deserve the spotlight and do you give them in the appropriate order? Does your presentation draw people's attention in such a way that they remember the key points and want to stay involved? How about your conclusion—do you make it clear what you want people to do?

Next, your group presentation skills—how good are you in front of a group? It has been said that the number one human fear is speaking in front of a group. Is it for you? I personally am quite

---

CASE STUDY

Pay Phones

According to an AT&T study of public pay phones, many branded pay phones in the same locale as an independent pay phone generate over 250% more traffic. Customers will even wait for the branded phone to come free while the unbranded phone sits idle. The reason? Over time, pay phone users have learned (or been told) that charges at independent pay phones can be much higher than charges at recognized brands such as AT&T or Bell Atlantic. If pay phone users knew the tariffs, they would probably use the closest or cheapest pay phone, regardless of brands.

CASE STUDY

Los Angeles Dodgers

In order to increase the number of games that children attend and to educate them about baseball, the Los Angeles Dodgers have created 'Kids' Clubhouse.' The Dodgers believe the increasing amount of sports entertainment available is diluting the potential fan base of baseball. More children today play soccer than any other organized activity. In order to get kids "into the game," 'Kids' Clubhouse' provides children with an inside look into America's pastime. Autograph sessions with players, on-field practices with coaches, and stadium tours provide kids with a much stronger understanding of the nuances of baseball.

---

comfortable doing it, but I have friends who are terrified by the prospect.

So think about your skill in group presentations. If your skill is good, but your confidence is low, you won't be very effective. If you're confidence is good, but your skill is low, you'll be boring and ineffective. So work on both your skill and your confidence level.

Next, look at your success ratio when you're forced to sell through other people, instead of selling in person, by yourself.

Now, when I say sell through others, I mean someone says, "OK, give me your information and I'll take it to the decision maker." When you are in a situation like that, how effective can you be? That happens to lots of us. There are many times when we're not able to be the one who gives the sales presentation to the person who makes the buying decision.

Learn what to do, learn how to develop your materials and your delivery, how to cultivate the relationships with the right people, and how to follow through appropriately so that, when you must sell through others, they truly want to buy.

Finally, how good are you at adjusting your presentation style to fit different customers? Can you speed up or slow down effectively? Do you know how to summarize and get to the key points, or expand and add more depth, with confidence? Do you know how to focus on the things customers care about when those aren't the things at the top of their list, even if you feel that they should be? How do you still make your point and get them to feel truly concerned about the things you think they should be concerned about, when it's obvious that there's primarily something else on their mind?

These things can be done. The better you know yourself and know how well you're able to do these things, the more you can learn to focus on each and become more effective at it.

See the Meaning in What You Do

The Criticality of Solving Problems

Ted Levitt, editor of the Harvard Business Review, said, "At their core, products are problem-solving tools. People buy products if they fulfill a problem-solving need."

"Waiter, could I have some more
water right away?"

Always solve the customer's
main problem first.

I believe the purpose of business is to make life better for people. How do you make life better for people? Any business that doesn't do this will soon be out of business. All it takes is one good competitor and all your accounts are in jeopardy.

Consider the impact of what you do on those that you do it for. In what ways does buying from you or doing business with you make someone else's life better? Take some time to write out your answer. Seriously, write this out, because the more clear it is in your mind, the more clear it will be in their mind as they listen to you.

One day I was in the Atlanta Airport, walking through the area called the Food Court, where there are several serving stations and one seating area. It was jam-packed with people, a very busy day. I got a cup of coffee and watched the people. All the seats were filled so I didn't try to compete for a seat. I was watching a bus boy as he roamed between the tables cleaning up the trash left by each of the guests. This guy was so depressed, he was slumped over, he had a long face, he looked very unhappy. He would drag himself from table to table as he cleaned up the messes and he never made eye contact with anybody.

After a moment or two I discarded my coffee cup in the trash receptacle, walked over to him and said, "Excuse me." He backed up like he thought I was going to be chewing him out or somehow he was going to get in trouble. "I'd just like to make an observation," I said. "What you're doing sure makes a difference here." He said, "What?" I said, "Look at this place, if you weren't cleaning these tables, within five minutes there'd be trash everywhere." He said, "I know." I said, "So what you're doing really makes a difference here, I just thought I'd say thanks for doing it." Then I walked away.

When I was about ten feet way, I glanced back. I swear this guy looked like he had grown six inches. He was standing a little bit taller, he was making eye contact occasionally with people. Now he didn't burst into the mode of "Service Man" and all of a sudden go gleefully hopping from table to table. But what he did is go from a depressed body language to neutral body language, showing neither happiness nor sadness.

But what do you bet for the balance of his shift he did his work a little better? What do you bet for the balance of his shift that day he felt a little better about himself, and he probably even handled problems more smoothly?

Now the question would be, if that was the case, what in the world did I do to cause that effect on him? All I did really was point out how the work he was doing made life better for other people. I showed him how it made his work station a better place to be, a healthier place to be, a more sanitized and a more pleasant-looking place to be. But most of all what I did was give him back his dignity. I showed him there was a purpose in what he was doing, not merely a process of drudgery that he had to perform.

When we see purpose in what we do, we do what we do more effectively. When we see no purpose in it, it feels like slavery. When we see a purpose in it, it feels like meaningful behavior, meaningful activity.

Many years ago, Victor Frankl, who survived the Holocaust as a prisoner of war during WWII, wrote a book called *Man's Search For Meaning*. In it he told about how people had endured the most horrible of horrible experiences in those death camps. The ones who endured it and survived were the ones who had a sense of purpose, a sense of meaning, a reason for staying alive.

That's a very dramatic and powerful illustration of the need for meaning. But even on a simple day-to-day basis, like the case with the busboy in the airport, all of us need a sense of meaning in what we do. We need to understand the why, not merely the how of what we do.

The Structure of Effective Presentations

Let's talk about making a sales presentation. Although many salespeople like to wing it, rather than prepare a structured presentation, the majority of professionals rely on an outline. They practice some of the lines that they speak over and over throughout the years and they become very adept at delivering those specific words in their own personal way, knowing that their presentation will have impact when delivered in the manner they've perfected.

Whether you speak well, or not, you still must give a logical flow to your ideas. In your presentation, be sure to cover five general areas.

1. **The claim.** You're making a presentation, so what is your claim? What benefit are you going to bring to people? Increased sales, fewer sick days, less paperwork, fewer mechanical breakdowns, greater life opportunities, more free time? Whatever it is, it must be related to your prospect's

need, the gap they feel between what they've got and what they'd like to have.

2. **The need gap.** Over half your work as a salesperson is going to be focused on uncovering and diagnosing each person's need gap. During a presentation what you have to do is keep him or her aware of the gap between what they have and what they want, and continually show how your product or service fills that gap.

3. **The solution.** Your product or service has to genuinely solve the prospect's problem. You have to present a clear, concise statement of how your product will do it, and you may include specific measurable criteria by which the success of the solution can be judged. This could be a point of negotiation, or it may ultimately reflect a guarantee that comes with your product or service. But the solution has to be clear, and your prospects have to be confident that you can provide it.

4. **Documentation.** How can you prove your claim, how can you show that you really will provide that benefit? Offer testimonial letters, be specific, give an impressive demonstration, present slides, show pictures, graphs, data, other proof, use brochures. Call someone else on your cell phone and have them give an on-the-spot testimonial in the midst of the sales presentation. Do a conference call, do an online video presentation in which you're able to use visuals and have several people on the call at the same time, each interacting from their own computer.

5. **A call to action.** You've got to ask for the sale. Too many salespeople don't do this, and it's a natural thing to ask for feedback on your presentation and your product or service; but it's also a natural thing to ask them to make a decision. "If you don't ask, you don't get."

To be more effective in making presentations, here are a few key tips.

- **Be entertaining or interesting.** Do what you do in such a way that it draws other people in and gathers their attention. Remember Murphy's Law: "Whatever can happen, will happen, and probably at the worst possible moment." Do your preparation, cover the little details, make sure that everything that can be prepared for has been prepared for.

- **Play off needs.** When you're talking with a customer, talk in terms of what they need, what they care about, what they're concerned about. Keep it relevant.

- **Customize your presentation, follow a structure, only discuss the features of your product or service** that are related to the interest of that prospect. Don't try to educate them about all the features. And convert the features into benefits to them. Be ethical, don't exaggerate, tell them the truth, if you don't know the answer to a question, say, "I don't know the answer to that, but I'll check it out and I'll get back to you."

- **Build perceived value.** Show them, by the way you propose a solution, that you know their buying criteria and what will make this a successful decision for them. Address both of these, the buying criteria and the success criteria.

- **Differentiate yourself from your competition.** Show how you stand out. What's better about doing business with you? Be confident, state your case with conviction, believe in it, share your enthusiasm, don't try to hold back. Stay sensitive to your prospect's needs, though, listen to what they're saying to you, watch their body language and their reactions, adapt to them.

- **Create carefully worded phrases** over time that you can use again and again to say the most vital parts of your sales presentation in the perfect way for you. Present simple, broad concepts first, complex detailed concepts later in the presentation. Lay the groundwork, then get specific.

- **Customize your presentation to the behavioral style, the personality of the person you're dealing with.** Ask for feedback constantly throughout your presentation. Don't make it a lecture, make it a dialogue, involve your prospect.

Believe in what you do, show your belief, and be prepared. It will be contagious and they will buy from you.

Let the Customer Sell Himself

Many years ago, professional sales trainer Fred Herman had the opportunity to appear on a television interview show hosted by Mike Douglas. Before the show he was screened by one of the show's producers and the following exchange took place. The producer said, "Mr. Herman, so you're a sales expert? If you're so good at selling, sell me something."

Fred said, "What would you like me to sell you?"

The producer said, "Sell me that ashtray."

Fred said, "Why would you want that ashtray?"

The producer said, "It's a needed item in this office, we've got a lot of smokers and it helps keep the office clean."

Fred asked, "What other reasons would you have for wanting that ashtray?"

The producer said, "The colors fit our color scheme, it's about the right size."

Fred then asked, "What do you think that ashtray is worth?"

The producer said, "About twenty dollars."

Fred said, "Well, I guess I'll let you buy it."

By asking the appropriate questions, Fred was able to lead the producer through an evaluation of the product, in the light of his or her own needs, and when the producer saw how the product met his needs, agreed on a reasonable price for it, there was no selling to be done. The customer literally had sold himself.

How could you use this technique to do part of your selling?

"Want a Catalog?"

One European business equipment firm with twenty thousand customers simply went back over its records for the past two years and discovered that its top three thousand customers had given it more than fifty percent of its orders. So, instead of mailing out quarterly catalogs to every customer, the firm now sends custom catalogs to these three thousand customers, following up with a phone call. It sends annual catalogs to the middle ten thousand customers, and it sends postcards to the bottom seven thousand who haven't ordered anything in the past two years ("Want a catalog? Send in this postcard."). The increased cost of treating high-value customers better is more than paid for by the reduced cost of providing fewer services to low-value accounts.

Rescuing Customers from Competitors

Why don't you rescue some people from your competitors? That's right. I'm talking about going and getting customers to leave your competitors and come to you.

In some industries that's not appropriate, but in most industries it's as common as going to work in the morning. How do you win your competitors' customers? Converting customers from competitors is a fact of life for many salespeople. Sometimes customers become dissatisfied and they switch. Sometimes they switch because geographic moves or other needs have emerged. Your market share will increase if they come to you and decrease if they go to your competitor.

Here are some ways to entice your prospects to switch to you:

1. **Think long-term.** Don't give up when you hear them say, "I'm satisfied." Satisfaction may be temporary, their needs might change, or you might come up with a good reason for them to switch.

2. **Develop a relationship.** Cultivate a business friendship with each of these prospects. By developing this friendship you'll be able to do item three.

3. **Study their needs.** Take your time, do research, ask non-threatening questions so that you can find out what your prospect needs and how well they're being satisfied currently. The key is to find a need gap and then offer a solution.

4. **Sell yourself.** Personal chemistry is important, but so is knowledge that shows you're enthusiastic, earnest, professional, ethical and a caring expert, who will be an asset to do business with. Come up with new ideas for your prospects even if they're not doing business with you. Give them good ideas, show them you care, show them you're on their team. Sale or no sale, earn the right to get some of their business.

5. **Add value.** Many products or services are so common that they're commodities. Differentiation may be difficult; it might be that someone else offers virtually the same, or maybe even exactly the same products that you offer. But, they don't offer *you*. That's why you have to sell yourself into this equation, emphasizing such things as extra touches, performance guarantees, superior service, better delivery schedules, or whatever it takes, within reason.

6. **Ask for a no-risk trial order.** Say, "Just give me a chance to show you what I can do." Many customers are loyal to their suppliers, but they'll grant you a trail order if you ask for it. Make it a no-risk deal. Ensure that they will be satisfied through some kind of guarantee and then bend over backwards to make sure the trial order makes a very positive impression—give them a sample of what they can get from you.

7. **Ask them for a portion of their business.** Converting a competitor's customer may not be an all-or-nothing deal. You may be able to do it bit by bit. Prove yourself slowly as you

go along, just get a small percentage of their business and then let that grow into something larger.

8. **Be persistent.** Nothing succeeds like persistence. All things being equal, the salesperson who's persistent will win the account just about every time. Keep in touch with prospects, think long-term, be a consultant and an ally, and you will plant drought-resistant seeds. In other words, these people will stick with you through the hard times. But what you've got to do is persist in a way that's appealing and professional, not in a way that's annoying.

They say sometimes it takes five or ten calls to make a sale. Well, if all five or ten of those calls are just you coming by one more time to beg, plead, or harangue the person for business, you're going to become an annoyance and you're not likely to get the sale ever.

However, if every time you make a contact, you learn a little bit more about them, every time you make a contact you bring them one simple idea, one little insight, or one bit of information that makes them more effective—over time you become, not only their business friend, but a subject expert whom they respect. Once you are their subject expert, you can become their preferred provider.

How to Sell through Others

Do you ever have to sell through others? When you meet a potential buyer, it's important to determine whether you're talking with the person who actually makes the buying decision or not. You might just ask, who usually makes buying decisions for your company? If the reply is, "I screen the products and recommend the top two or three to a final decision maker," then you know that you will have to make two sales—one, to your contact, and two, to their supervisor or the decision maker.

Your contact will become your sales representative. Think about that, *if they're carrying your message to someone else, they are your salesperson in that organization. So it's imperative to prepare your contact well to represent you and your product or service.* If you don't take the time to prepare them, you reduce your chances of a sale.

First, outline the key points that you want them to make and then summarize the main reasons why that organization should buy from you.

Second, include enough copies of your sales materials so that each person who's in on the discussion has his or her own copy. A little bit of added expense in putting together special packages for each individual may greatly assist your likelihood of getting a sale.

Third, highlight key points of your product or service that make it different from those of competitors, and put those points in writing.

Here are some important questions to answer before you attempt to sell through someone else.

- Where does the decision maker get his or her information?
- If there's more than one decision maker, in what sequence are decisions like this made?
- Who reports to whom?
- In the case of a committee, who will present your ideas to the group, and who has the most authority on that committee?
- If you were contacted by the prospect, did the prospect initiate the contact? Or, was he or she asked to contact you by somebody else? A lot of times we find that they're not the buyer at all, someone else just asked them to gather some information.
- Who, besides the decision maker, influences the choices that are made?
- What does the buyer really want and need?

When someone else is carrying your message, he or she is your sales rep. Take the time to give them a brief moment of training and the tools with which to do the selling effectively. You'll increase your likelihood of gaining a "yes."

■ ■ ■

THE SIXTH COMPETENCY

Commit
Confirm That a Purchase Has Been Made

The Benefit Summary

ONE OF THE MOST OVERLOOKED ASPECTS OF SELLING IS GIVING A SUMMARY of the benefits toward the end of the buying process—reviewing with the customer all the benefits that will come to him or her if they say yes to you today.

In the benefit summary, the points to which they have responded positively are summarized. So you go over the benefits, not just the features of your product or service. There's a big difference. This is especially important if your prospect takes the information back to another decision maker.

When this is the case, your prospect becomes your salesperson, he or she is representing you. So you must prepare the prospect well to represent you and your company to the next person in the decision-making line. Leave as little as possible to their memory, put everything in writing and provide them with collateral materials, if possible.

The same thing applies when you're not dealing with the one individual in front of you. You will know what benefits to emphasize by noting your prospect's reactions throughout the presentation, what they liked and didn't, and by the data that you've gathered during your information gathering before you made the call.

One way to involve your prospects in your presentation is to have them create their own list of benefits. Get them to imagine how they would use your product or service, and what benefits would come to them, and then ask them to list those themselves. That will cause a person to sell himself.

You can accomplish this by asking how your product or service will help him or her with a specific problem. After he or she tells you the benefit, ask what other problems this would address.

The benefit summary encapsulates your presentation highlights; it's an opportunity to ask for feedback and a way to help your prospect retain the most important points. When you present your benefit summary, list the most important items first and last; they're the ones that stick in their mind the longest. In other words, you start the presentation of the benefit summary by reviewing the items that appeal to them most. Then you go through the other items. Finally, you summarize by focusing once again on the most appealing items.

Once agreement has been expressed, the buying signals should turn green for you. The language of a benefit summary is fairly simple. You might say, "Mr. Rush, we've talked about many things in the last hour, let me summarize what I see as the benefits for you."

Let's say you're selling a car. "You're looking for a car that will bring you prestige. You said you want something that will travel smoothly at highway speeds, and you also mentioned that you want something small for easy parking. And then you said it was important for you to be the first person on your block to have one because you don't like having the same car that everyone else has. Is that pretty accurate?"

Then he says "yes" or gives you a correction.

And you say, "Based on all of those things, seeing that this car is unique and it's new to the market, you're likely to be the first one in your neighborhood to have one. It is, as we've seen, small enough for ease of parking, travels smoothly at highway speeds. And it is a prestigious car, it's one that when people see it they respect the buyer of the car as someone of substance. Based on these things, why don't we go ahead and get started today?"

When you summarize what really matters most to them, you have stimulated the feelings that will cause them to say, "I'll take it."

Confirming versus Closing the Sale

Traditional salespeople study closing techniques as a way of building up their arsenal of weapons for the sales battle.

Relationship Selling salespeople see the sales effort as a cooperative effort, not as a battle. They study closing techniques, but they do it to give themselves various options to use with different types of people in different situations. It's part of maintaining a smooth working relationship—selling to someone the way they want to be sold and making the buying process easy for the customer.

Traditional salespeople think of the close as a series of techniques used at the end of a presentation. These techniques are designed to get the prospect to say yes and to give you an order, even if they don't want to.

Consultative sellers, the types that would use relationship selling, take a much more enlightened view of confirming the sale. They *don't think of it as closing anything. They see it as the opening or beginning of a relationship.* They think of it as a natural process, the logical outcome of involving the customer in every step of the sales process.

There are two ways to involve a prospect—the manipulative way and the nonmanipulative way. Traditional salespeople often ask questions that give the prospect frequent opportunities to say yes or no.

Some people believe that a prospect is more likely to say "Yes" if she has gotten in the habit of answering yes to a lot of small questions prior to that. It's a twisted game in which the salesperson wins agreement throughout the sales process, hoping that a lot of little yes's add up to a big yes. The problem is, the prospect answers yes to simple, superficial questions that don't necessarily build an argument in favor of the sale.

Other salespeople think prospects have a need to say "no." By giving them the opportunity to say no to a lot of questions, the thinking goes, the prospect will have the no's out of their system and be ready to say yes when the salesperson asks for the sale.

Both of these tactics are silly. The real way to involve a prospect is to make sure the two of you are on the same wavelength all the time. The ideal sales process is a mutual journey of uncovering a need, working on a solution, and confirming a decision to buy. When the journey is mutual, then confirming the sale is a matter of *when*, not *whether*, they're going to buy. When the journey is not mutual, the salespeople spend their time trying to convince prospects that they need something that's being sold and the sales process can become the type of unethical arm twisting that everyone hates and that salespeople have many times been blamed for doing.

For the nonmanipulative salesperson, the one who practices Relationship Selling, the sale begins when a customer says yes. It's the start of an ongoing business relationship.

Think about the analogy of confirming the sale and of asking someone to marry you. If you were going to ask someone whether they would marry you, and you didn't know whether they would say "yes" or "no," it's not the time to ask. Obviously the question would be premature. The decision to marry is the outcome of a mutually developed relationship. Usually the issue has been discussed before the question is formally asked. When it's asked, it's almost a rhetorical question. And it's simply crystallizing a discussion that's gone before. If it's a total surprise, and you're not sure what the answer's going to be, maybe now is not the time to ask.

The same thing is true in a selling situation. Confirming the sale is simply getting commitment to go ahead.

So always look for ways to come to a decision together, to confirm a commitment, not simply close a sale.

Resistance—Objections Are Feedback

One of the biggest areas of concern in sales training has been handling objections. In the old industrial-era mindset, we used to look at objections as a barrier that had to be fought over until somebody won. It was a battle of ping-pong, more or less, back and forth across the net. The person serves you an objection and you respond with a creatively crafted response, which causes this person to want to buy, supposedly. It goes back and forth until either they run out of objections, or you run out of crafty responses.

First off, let's get rid of objections altogether. If there's an objection, things have gone too far in a negative direction. Deal with objections while they're still merely concerns.

Concerns are feedback. When you hear an expression of a concern, don't take that to mean, "I'm not going to buy." Just take it to mean, "I'm not sold yet." There's a big difference. Very few sales proceed from start to finish with the customer agreeing one hundred percent on every point.

Similarly, few customers disagree with one hundred percent of what you say, so somewhere in between those extremes are the give and take, the percentages that represent today's sales contact. You will have a much healthier attitude and healthier sales behavior if you welcome the resistance you get, rather than fear it. Welcome it as a form of feedback.

Let's take a look at what you do now to uncover resistance. Recall a recent unsuccessful sales attempt when you handled the prospect's resistance poorly or ineffectively. What was your customer's concern? Write it down or think about it. How did you respond? How might you have answered more effectively, now that you have a chance to reflect on it?

When someone tells you they think that your price is too high, how do you respond to that?

When a prospect has doubts about the quality of your product, or about your company's reputation, maybe they haven't heard of you. What do you say? Do you become defensive? Does it show up in your tone?

On a scale of one to ten, rate yourself on the qualities needed when dealing with customer resistance:

- Your confidence level when they resist
- Your confidence in your company or your product
- Your product knowledge
- Your knowledge of your industry
- Your knowledge of human nature, personality differences
- Your ability to avoid an argument and still achieve a result
- Your calmness under stress
- Your ability to be diplomatic

Each of these is an area you could cultivate to become more effective in dealing with resistance. So take a look at what you do now, and that will tell you what you need to do to be more effective in the future.

Why Customers Resist and What to Do about It

Why is it customers resist buying? Well, actually customers don't resist. *Customers love to buy. Everybody loves to buy. We just don't like to be sold.* We don't like others convincing us to buy. We like to buy because we want to. So what would cause someone to resist? There are many reasons:

- ▦ **No need.** Maybe what they need is different from what you're offering, or they don't see the connection between what you're offering and what they feel that they need.

- ▦ **No trust.** Maybe they just don't know you well enough yet to trust you. Or maybe they don't know your company or your product, or your type of product well enough to trust it.

- ▦ **No authority.** Maybe they don't have the clout, the position, the written authority, the formal authority, to make such a sales commitment.

- ▦ **Or maybe it's just their ability.** Maybe they don't have the money or the resources to commit to it, or the time.

So it's no need, no trust, no authority, no ability, or maybe you have the wrong product or wrong features. Maybe what you're offering is close, but not quite what they're looking for. Maybe it's too small, too large, too much, too little, too soon, too late. It could be any number of things. Maybe it's the wrong price, maybe they can't afford to buy what they truly want or truly need. So you have to find a way to help them acquire a little of it and then grow to a larger commitment to it.

It's also conceivable that the issue of price is a cover-up. Sometimes they can say it costs too much and what they really mean is, "No, I think my boss would be mad if I bought this."

There are types of resistance. There's valid resistance, which is legitimate; they actually don't have the resources, or they have a valid reason for not saying yes to you. There's not much of a way out of that one. If the resistance is genuine, if there is not a good reason for them to go ahead, they should not go ahead.

But then again, more often than not, the resistance is a smoke-screen. It's what we call invalid resistance. They say, "Leave your material with me, I'll look it over when I get a chance." Or, "I'm going to have to discuss this with my partner, my wife, my boss, or somebody else." And maybe that's the case. However, a lot of times they're telling you that just to get rid of you.

Invalid objections pose a challenge to your attitude. Your positive attitude must be conveyed as you handle the resistance. For example, you could say, "I understand you're busy, so may I see you this afternoon or tomorrow morning when you've got more free time?" Or, "I don't mind leaving some materials with you, I'll be happy to do that, but I get the impression you're still unclear on some aspect of what we just discussed. Is there a point I might add a little bit more to that might make you feel more comfortable with going ahead?"

Or, "I don't blame you for wanting to involve your partner, your wife, your boss in this decision. Let's ask her to join us now for a moment and we'll bring her up to speed."

To find out the real reason behind resistance, use the following four-step process for handling resistance:

1. Listen carefully, don't interrupt them, hear them out.

2. Check your understanding by giving feedback, such as, "Let me see if I understood you properly, here's what I hear you saying, is that accurate?"

3. Address the issue effectively, use logic and emotion. In other words, talk about the feelings, but also talk about the logic.

4. Confirm the acceptance of your solution. If you handled it well, it shouldn't be an issue any longer. So ask, "Does that put your concerns to rest?"

Once you've dealt with the resistance, you may be in a position to ask for the sale. So when do you respond to resistance? The best time is before it even comes up.

Every product or service has strengths and weaknesses. Knowing your weaknesses and having an answer built into your presentation is a very smart thing to do. Handle it before it comes up. That also allows you to keep things in perspective. So list for yourself three common issues that customers bring up that represent a potential weakness. And then write down exactly what you can say in response to build confidence in your product.

Another time to respond to resistance is immediately. Customers don't want to be ignored. So when they bring something up, address it. Unless you have a logical reason to postpone your answer, handle the resistance immediately. It shows that you're in control, that you're confident, and you know what you're talking about.

If you have to delay a response, you might say to them, "I'll address that in just a second. Let me make one other key point, and then I'll address your concern."

The third time to respond to resistance is later, after postponing. This could be a matter of just choosing the right timing in your presentation to address the key issues. You might say, "That's an important question, but one I'd like to cover in a few minutes, if you don't mind. I want to put this in perspective so the price will have some meaning to you, is that OK?" Stay tuned to their responses, keep on track with your presentation, and you'll build confidence in your sale.

The company always liked to take a Good Rep,
Bad Rep approach to sales calls.

Handling "It Costs Too Much"

What do you do when someone says, "Your product or service costs too much?" When they say, "It's too expensive," how do you handle that objection? Actually, if you treat it as an objection, you immediately put yourself in a combative posture with the customer. What I would suggest is that you treat it, as I've said many times, as a concern. *What does "It's too expensive," or "It costs too much" really mean?*

There is not a universal meaning. It means different things to different people, at different times. Your first task is to figure out what they meant by it. Someone says, "It costs too much," and you say, "Costs too much in what way?"

They say, "It exceeds our budget for this year."

There they have told you that it's a budgetary limitation that you're dealing with. They're concerned with exceeding this year's budget. So what can you do? One, look for another line item

CASE STUDY

A Moving Experience

A salesperson for a moving company tells this story about handling "it costs too much":

"I was assigned to see a family that was moving from Cleveland to Los Angeles, all the expenses to be paid by their employer. They had already signed up with another company at a much lower price than I ever could quote. Undaunted, however, I pressed on. At the end of my presentation to the woman of the house, I was never more astonished in my career than when she announced that she would switch the job to us and pay the difference out of her own pocket. I couldn't help asking her what I said that had caused her to change movers.

She answered: "When you told me how the movers would carry those special containers you have with our clothes in them up to the rooms in my new house wearing gloves, and when you pictured for me how nice and fresh and wrinkle-free the clothes would look when they came out of the special containers, and I realized how much time and money and hassle I would save in laundry and dry cleaning—well, that was when I decided to let you handle our move.""

within the existing budget where you can get the money, or, two, look at the next budgeting cycle and get it built into the program for next year's budget.

Someone might come back by saying, "That's more money than I've ever spent for something like this." In this case, your prospect may simply be feeling resistant, a reluctance to commit because of the size of the purchase. Here you could respond by talking about the fact that the benefits far outweigh this extra commitment that they're making.

It might be that when they say, "It costs too much," they're talking about the product not being worth what you're charging. "I could get this same kind of a product for twenty percent less by just going down the street."

They're telling you to show them how the other alternatives will not fill their needs as well as your suggestion will. So you're in a balance sheet kind of a situation, showing their product or their other alternative versus your product or your possibilities. It's a matter of weighing values.

They might say, "I don't think my wife would go along with it, or I don't think my boss would go for it." In other words, "I'm not in this alone, I'm not the only decision maker, I need somebody else's approval. Unless you can convince me that this is a good enough idea that I can justify it to other people, then I'm probably not going to commit today."

They might say, "I don't mind the overall price. What bothers me is really the monthly payment seems pretty high." That's a matter of financing and terms.

Or they might say, "The payment is OK, but the overall price is so much." In that case you need to put that overall price in the right context for them so that they can see that by being able to afford it on a monthly basis, they'll also be able to justify it on an overall cost basis.

They might say, "It's going to take too much time, too many resources, too much energy on our part to put this into practice." Actually they're not resisting the price as much as they are the overall costs. Or the purchase is threatening their peace of mind by seeming to represent even more work to them.

Sometimes people say, "I'd rather not buy right now." In other words, it has nothing to do with the costs, it might be something that you missed earlier in the sales dialogue. Maybe you didn't connect with them well enough that they feel comfortable with you yet. Maybe you didn't find out enough about them to convince them you truly understand what their needs are and are recommending the right thing.

Maybe the way you made your presentation was so one-sided and seemingly manipulative, that they don't trust that you have their best interest in mind.

But when someone says, "It's too expensive, it costs too much," just recognize that that's the beginning of a new path of discovery on your part, so that you're able to understand the situation and the person even better, and to make recommendations and show value that will get them to go ahead today to say, "You're right, that's a good idea, I'll take it."

Recognizing Buying Signals

Do you know how to recognize buying signals? Buying signals are opportunities for you to confirm the commitment to the sale. The key to recognizing these opportunities is to know your prospect. By the time you get toward the end of your sales presentation, you should be familiar with this person's behavioral style, other personality traits they possess, and how they will respond to various ideas. This knowledge will help you understand the signals they're sending—buying signals or not-buying signals.

Always be sensitive to the prospect's needs. If you're in the middle of a presentation and you get cues that it's time to ask for the order, do so. But make sure that you've created sufficient perceived value in your prospect's mind. In other words, don't just ask them to say yes, do it in a way that shows you're sure that they have justification for making that decision, that they've thought it through, so they have some documentation that they can depend on it being a good decision. Condense your presentation, don't just stop abruptly. Give a quick benefit summary and then ask for the order. Find out what's needed and provide it.

It helps to be able to recognize a prospect's verbal and nonverbal buying signals. These come in three types. Think of a traffic light—red, yellow, and green. Red would be the stop light, that's a negative signal. It says, "I'm not ready to buy." Yellow would be neutral or caution, that says, "I'm not sure, I haven't made up my mind yet." And green, of course, is go, and that means, "I'm positive about this, I'm pleased, I'm interested in buying."

Listen to questions your prospects might ask. Sometimes they're good indicators of their mindset. And learn to interpret the questions and comments within the context of what you're suggesting to the person. Some typical questions could be, on the positive side, green lights, "Could I try this one more time?" Or, "Is it possible to install this on a trial basis, could we get started now?" Or, "What kind of warranty or service contract comes with this?" Or, "What sort of credit terms are available?" Or, "How soon could you deliver?" Those are all positive signals.

Here are some questions that would indicate caution, or the yellow light. "Is this system more reliable than mine?" Or, "This is interesting, what else could you tell me?" Or, "Can you leave some catalogue sheets with me so I can go over them with my colleagues?"

And here are some red light negative signals, some that tell you the person is not ready to buy. "I can't consider this with interest rates being as high as they are." Or, "Will these prices still be good, say, six months or a year from now?" Or, "You know, I'm overstocked now, where am I going to put more merchandise anyway?"

These signals give you an idea of where you stand. If the person gives you yellow signals, then they're still undecided. Perhaps you haven't given them enough information or the right kind of information yet that shows them the true value and the safety in saying yes to you.

When the buying signals are red, it's time to back up a step or two. Give a benefit summary, which is always a good transition, and politely ask an open-ended question with direction indicated, such as, "Where do we go from here?" or "What's our next step?" When you get negative signals, the main thing to do is know that you are not yet ready to ask for the order. You need further information to know truly where the value is for this customer, you can show the link between your product or service and the value they will receive.

"Can't you wait until I finish my recommendation?"

Above and beyond the specific suggestions, remember to always stay tuned to what's happening in your prospect's mind. Here are some suggestions as to what to look for in their body language, the nonverbal messages:

■ A prospect who sits with open arms is usually receptive to your idea. If they suddenly cross their arms tightly, they're indicating defensiveness. When they're defensive, find out what's wrong, work on the relationship for a moment. Interest is usually shown by leaning forward, listening carefully and nodding in agreement. If they're doing this, they're with you.

■ A prospect who is supporting his head with one hand and gazing off, clearly has lost interest or may be thinking about one of your ideas, and you might want to provide them a moment or two to think it through.

■ People relax when they decide to buy; this is a key. When you see a sudden change in their behavior, physically, they may be indicating a change in their mental attitude. If they've been tense and all of a sudden they relax, they may have just made

167

the buying decision. If they've been relaxed and they get tense, they may have just decided against going ahead. Whenever you see the body language change, make sure that you explore it to see what just took place.

■ Happy, animated facial expressions usually show that a prospect is relating well to you. But make sure that they're relating well to the benefits of your product or service as well.

Buying signals, verbal and non-verbal are a great way for you to stay tuned to the person so that you know how to guide them to the best decision.

Ten Power Factors in Negotiations

Negotiation is one of the key selling skills about which many people are intimidated. *Negotiation is simply a dialogue between people. You're weighing pluses and minuses. You're looking at options, and finding the best solution for all people involved. It's one of the oldest skills used to gain desired results.* It's also a skill many people misunderstand and find intimidating. But negotiation is simply the way we interact with others to compare offers and relative value and analyze our decisions.

Three factors that affect negotiation, according to negotiating expert Herb Cohen, are power, information, and time. The person with the most power has an edge. The person with the most information has an edge. The person with the most flexibility of time has an edge.

A few years ago I had the opportunity to work with Dr. James Hennig in the authoring of a program called *Negotiating Your Success*. Dr. Hennig is a specialist in negotiation and he identified ten factors that affect power in negotiation. Let me go over them with you.

1. **Alternative power.** The one who has the most alternatives usually wins. So know what your alternatives are and know

what the opposition's alternatives are, and be prepared in advance to explore those alternatives.

2. **Legitimacy power.** What kind of credibility do you have? Do you have the power that comes from a great track record? What has your past performance been? Do you have power that comes from referrals—either other people are saying great things about you or you have people in power positions who are lending you their power by saying that you're a good person? Do you have title power, an office or a position, an academic degree or license, an award or an honor that gives you an edge? All of these fall under legitimacy power.

3. **Risk power.** Who's most at risk here? Can you afford to have this negotiation fail? Can they?

4. **Commitment power.** What is the demonstrated commitment behind the position? In other words, the person who's made more of a commitment to his or her position has more power. But then again, the person who's made more of a commitment to their position is less likely to be flexible, so they have fewer alternatives. What you don't know can hurt you, so find out what kind of commitments have already been made.

5. **Knowledge power.** The more you know, the more options you see. The more options you see, the more possibilities lie before you. The more possibilities you have, the more likely you are to succeed. There's topic knowledge, knowing specifically about the topic on which you're negotiating. There's negotiation knowledge, knowing about negotiating itself and being able to handle negotiations intelligently. And there's opposition knowledge, in other words, knowing the other party, your competition; the more you know about them the better you're prepared to deal with them.

6. **Expert power.** When you lack knowledge personally, sometimes you can bring in an expert or refer to an expert source and gain power that way.

7. **Reward or punishment power.** The ability to reward or punish provides power in negotiation.

8. **Time or deadline power.** Personally you should try not to have a deadline, but definitely know the opposition's deadline. When their deadline is approaching and yours is not, you have more flexibility, thereby more power.

9. **Perception power.** Sometimes, it's not the person who has the power who has the edge, but the one who is *perceived* to have the most power.

10. **Relationship power.** Negotiating is not about beating the other person into submission. Negotiation is about connect-

"One small sticking point: Who's going to handle product delivery costs?"

ing with the other person and reaching a decision in such a way that both of you are happy with the outcome. When the relationship is good, details rarely get in the way.

My friend Dr. Tony Alessandra often says, "When two people want to do business together, the details won't keep them apart. But if two people do not want to do business together, the details will not confirm the deal."

The Pilot Program and the Puppy Dog Sale

Many years ago when I was first being trained as a salesperson, they taught me what was known at the time as, "the puppy dog close."

This was the technique of getting someone to say "yes" to a sale by agreeing to take home your product on a free trial basis. The analogy to the puppy dog is as if a person had stopped into a pet store where they saw a little puppy and they were debating in their mind whether they wanted to purchase the puppy and make it part of their family, or whether they wanted to pass on the decision and wait until a later time. What the store owner would often do is say, "Here, let me hand you the puppy." The person would start holding and cuddling the cute little puppy. Then the owner'd say, "Why don't you just take it home tonight and let it see your home and let your family get to know the puppy. Then if you don't want him, just bring him back tomorrow."

Now what's going to happen? You're going to take the puppy home, you're going to walk into the house with it, everybody's going to be excited and they're all going to want to hold the puppy and play with it. The entire family is going to put their focus on this puppy overnight. Then someone in the family, or some neighbor is going to say, "Oh, you have a puppy! What's its name?"

Well, trust me, when you come up with a name for it, it's family, it's there to stay and there's no way you're going to take it back to the store the next morning.

Art on Trial

One evening, my wife, Paula, and I had a few minutes before our dinner reservation at a local restaurant so we wandered into an art gallery. The salesperson noticed us admiring a piece of art and inquired about our interest. When he was convinced we were likely buyers, he asked, "Would you like to take it home for the weekend to see how it fits into your home?"

I quickly said, "No thanks." However, to my surprise, Paula said, "Yes!"

Well, once it was hanging over our fireplace, we both fell in love with it. The idea of returning it never crossed our minds. We called to confirm the sale and still enjoy the painting today, many years later.

The same thing is true for trying out a new piece of equipment. Not on the same emotional level, but it works as a fundamental principle. When you take it home, or you bring it into your office, you install it. When you start to experience the new product, you get accustomed to it in a new and different way. You see, *prior to taking this trial purchase, you were considering whether or not to buy. Once you begin the trial process, you are looking for reasons to reinforce your decision to say yes.*

This pilot project, allowing the customer to use and enjoy your product or service, is a very powerful form of convincing them that they've made the right decision. You could say, "Look, I can see you're undecided, why don't you take this quantity of them right now and see how you like them. If you like them, we'll do more business. If you don't, I'll take back those that were unused."

What happens is that the customer sees an easy, non-threatening way to get started with their commitment to buy. The right way to use the pilot confirmation is to assure that the customer is satisfied once a commitment exists. When a customer says to you, in essence, "If everything you said is true, then I think I want to buy." Offer them a trial run. It's an easy way to help a customer become comfortable with the commitment they want to make. In this situation their perception will be positive, and they will look for things that are right.

That's why a trial or a pilot is a powerful tool for assuring customer satisfaction, not just a technique for confirming a sale.

Timing—When to Ask for the Order

Salespeople often ask me, "If I'm in the middle of my presentation, and my prospect gives strong buying signals, should I stop and ask for the sale?"

The answer is "Yes, but no." You don't want to continue to the end of your presentation and risk boring your customer before you ask for the commitment. But then, you can't drop everything and just ask for the sale. Why? Because you have to create a perception of value in your prospect's mind by furnishing features and benefits that put everything in the proper perspective for them. So the key is to shorten your presentation, speed it up, and cut out any unnecessary or less important parts. Get to the most relevant points quickly and then ask for the commitment.

When should prices be revealed? Everybody comes into a situation wanting to know what a yes decision will cost them. Many times a customer will ask as their first comment to you, "What does it cost?" You can tell them what it costs and sometimes they'll just turn and walk away. I prefer to answer their question in a much broader context. In other words, instead of saying, "It costs $214," I say, "the cost of it depends on several key features." Then I focus on the features and ask them how that feature related to their need. And then I tell them what the price is. But only after I've pointed out the best features.

If a person, on the other hand, is impatient to get the price from you, what you want to do is tell them the price, but ask their permission to put that price in context. Say to them, "I'll tell you the price and I'd appreciate the opportunity to show you why that price makes good sense." And then explain the two or three key features that make this price a very good buy.

There are many ways to delay giving prices. The most honest way is to say, "With all due respect, the price, out of context, is meaningless, and doesn't carry any value to either of us. If you don't mind, I'll be happy to tell you about the price; but I'd like to tell you more about the product to put that price in the proper perspective."

You can also say, "There are a number of different plans available, I'd like to give you a better feel for our product or service and then you can see which plan suits you best. And I'll know exactly what the price would be for what you want to get."

If you sense that this is acceptable to the prospect, you can continue by asking some more information-gathering questions. Then quickly focus on the values that you can bring them. If they keep asking, offer a range of prices. The price can be between "X" and "Y." If they ask a third time, and it's getting to where you feel like this is a combat, then relax, and just tell them the price, and then talk about their needs.

It's better to risk telling the price too early than it is to risk making your prospect angry or suspicious of you. Giving a price before creating a sense of value in their mind is a disservice to the salesperson and to the customer. In a sense, the customer is then misled because he or she does not know what they're getting for the price, which makes the price meaningless. They're more apt to reject the product or service based on inadequate information.

At the same time, the salesperson is hindered from accurately presenting the product or service and loses sales as a result of the customer's lack of understanding. So, in order to give the price in the right context, always say, "The price for this benefit, this benefit, and this benefit is only," and then state the price.

Asking for the Sale

Ask for the order. If you don't ask people to buy, chances are really, really, really good they're not going to buy. A lot of times if you watch a salesperson, you will find that they operate by a different assumption. They make their presentation. They present all the appeals that they can offer. They build value and then they keep watching the customer, hoping the customer is going to take it away from them. That the customer is going to say, "Yes, I want to buy it," "OK, I'll take it," "Let's get started," or something like that. But *most customers want to be led. Customers want you to let them know when's the appropriate moment for them to commit to buying. If you don't ask for the sale, chances are good you won't get the sale.* Here are some ways to ask.

You could ask in a way that's very non-threatening, very indirect, what we would call an *assumptive sales confirmation.* This is generally using a trial commitment, questions that determine whether a prospect is ready to make a commitment. The assumption is not that you are going to force the sale; but that you and your prospect, have been, and continue to be, on the same wavelength. So the sale is a given.

Even so, assumptive confirmations must be used respectfully. Here's one, the alternate choice—this is where you pose two alternatives. Instead of between yes and no, they're *choosing* between yes and yes. "Do you want delivery made to your New York warehouse, or your New Jersey distribution center?" Either way, they're buying. "Do you want special terms or is our standard two percent in thirty days good enough for you? Do you want the standard service contract or would you like the more comprehensive coverage for this?"

Another way to use the alternate choice is to test the waters.

If the prospect's buying signals are unclear, you could say, "If you were going ahead with this today, would you want the modular office system or the custom-designed layout?" Notice, you're not asking them to make a commitment, you're asking them for an indication of interest: "Which of these is more interesting?"

Another is using a minor point. This seeks to get the prospect to answer a question about a minor detail of the product or service. If the question is answered, the assumption is that the sale is going to be made. It's not a very safe assumption unless buying signals are clearly positive. So nonmanipulative, relationship-oriented salespeople use minor points as stepping stones to confirming the sale, but with a slight twist from the traditional approach. *The questions are asked as a way to get the prospect to visualize owning the product or service, in their mind.* This is a part of information gathering and it's an effective way to get someone involved in the sales process. A question might be, "Where would you be using this cell phone the most? Would you be using it while traveling in your car? Would you be using it in a remote office, or would you be carrying it with you all the time?"

You could say, "Do you want to train your entire staff at one time, or do you want to train just a few at a time?" You could say, "Would you want your VIPs picked up at the airport in a limousine or would you prefer that we use our shuttle bus?"

Whenever you're presenting a minor point like this, you're getting the person to commit to a portion of the decision that constitutes the overall sale. We all know that a picture is worth a thousand words. So get your prospect to visualize the ownership and use of your product or service. Then you'll smooth the way for their acceptance of it.

Another technique would be *physical action*—to actually begin the buying process. You pull an order blank out and you start filling in the information, just assuming that you're going ahead. You'd use this technique only if the signals you're getting are clearly green, "go ahead" signals. Otherwise it's rude, insensitive, and absurd to ignore people's resistance and just continue writing up the sale.

So, as you pull out the order blank, do it early, and start filling in information as you go along. If the person says, "Hey, I haven't decided to buy yet," you say "fine, I'm just recording this information in the event you do decide to." Then you go right ahead.

Another way to ask for the order is the *direct confirmation*. There's nothing wrong with being straightforward, just confidently ask for the sale. It's the natural thing to do if you've covered all the points. But most salespeople neglect to ask for the sale.

Without fail, corporate buyers report that salespeople continually flop by being poor listeners and failing to ask for the sale. Fear of rejection is the only reason why someone would fail to ask for an order. If you've conducted the sales process in a consultative, relationship-oriented way, you don't have anything to fear. The communication is open, you understand the person, you've solved their problem by showing them the value they get from you, now is the time to ask for the sale.

Many buyers appreciate a no-nonsense approach. There is nothing wrong with saying, "May I have your business?" It's direct and it's polite. But be careful whom you use it with. People who are very direct and outgoing themselves appreciate it. People who are more reserved might feel a little intimidated by it. Whatever you do, avoid asking in a negative way, like, "*Why don't we* write up an order?" Or, "*Is there any reason why we shouldn't* go ahead?" That puts the emphasis on the negative factors, not the positive reasons for saying yes.

Instead say, "Let's set up your account for next week so you can start using this service as soon as possible." Or, "I have a truck coming into town this Thursday, I'll put your order on it, how's that?" Or, "I know you're going to be happy with this system, can I turn your order in today?"

Traditional salespeople often say something like, "What will

it take to get you to buy today?" That question is confronta-
tional. "What will it take?" First off, you're putting all the responsibility on the buyer. You're asking them to tell you how to
sell to them. They will ultimately tell you, but not in a direct
confrontation like that one. Instead, you might say, "How can I
help you today, what is it you're looking for most in an automobile?" Or you might say, "Glad to see you today, is there any particular model that you're interested in right now?" Or, "What
brought you in here today? This is a great day for buying a car."

All of those are positive, but none of them are confronta-
tional. Look for a way to ask for the sale whether you're greeting the person, summing up, or showing your product versus a
competitor's product. Ask for the sale, at the appropriate time, in
the appropriate way, and make it clear that the customer knows
that he or she is saying yes to a sale.

There's also the *act-now confirmation*. Telling your prospect
about, for example, a potential price increase or a promotional
special, can often motivate an undecided buyer and create a sense
of urgency. "Hey, my company has just announced that prices will
go up by five percent next month because of supplier increases. If
I can write your order up right now, you can stock up before this
increase takes effect." The act-now confirmation should only be
used when it is factual, when it's true. Don't use it deceptively.
When you're selling something they truly need, there's nothing
wrong with urging the person to act now to save time or money
or avoid inconvenience. This can do wonders for your reputation. You'll be a hero by saving them from the consequences of
not acting now.

So any time you're in a sales situation, be conscious of whether
you've asked for the order, and whether the customer *knows*
if you've asked for their business. Those who don't ask, don't get.
Those who do, make more sales.

■ ■ ■

THE SEVENTH COMPETENCY

Assure
See That the Customer
Remains Satisfied

The Value of Assuring Customer Satisfaction

I LOVE TO RIDE MOTORCYCLES. Several years ago I went into the motor-cycle dealership where I often do business and I found a pair of summer gloves that I wanted and bought them. They were in-expensive; I think they cost twenty-one dollars. I took them home and when I got them out of the package and tried them on, they didn't fit quite right.

So I took them back to the dealer the next day and I found a pair of gloves that were one dollar cheaper, and I said, "These gloves didn't quite fit me but these other gloves fit me quite well; they're not in a package, so I've already had the chance to try them on. Let's trade gloves and you just keep the extra dollar, I'm not inter-ested in a refund, I just want to get some gloves I can wear."

The guy behind the counter, whose name was Scott, said, "Do you have your receipt?" And I said, "No." He said, "Then I can't exchange them."

I said, "But you sold them to me yesterday."

He said, "I know, but I can't exchange them without a receipt. That's just the way we do it here."

So I said, "Well, let me talk to your manager."

So his manager came over and I told him what I wanted to do. And he said, "Do you have a receipt?" And I said, "Not on me, I have one at home."

"Jim," he said, "put yourself in my position. If someone comes in here like you, and they want to trade gloves, and they don't have a receipt, heck, these gloves could have fallen off a turnip truck."

And I said, "A glove truck maybe." He said, "OK, OK. But still, they might have stolen them or picked them up somewhere else. Without a receipt how do I know we sold them?"

I said, "Put yourself in my position. Scott here has sold me, not only these gloves, but many, many other things over the years. And you, personally, as a sales manager, sold me my last motorcycle, and it cost me over ten thousand dollars. Prior to your being here, I bought two other motorcycles from this dealership and barring any negative outcomes to today's dialogue, I'll probably buy future motorcycles here. So the best I can tell, I am not an annoyance to your business, or a potential threat, I'm an asset worth at least forty thousand dollars and maybe more to your dealership."

All of a sudden his body language changed, he looked a lot more pleasant and agreeable, and he said, "Would you like a bag for those gloves or do you just want to wear them home?"

His whole position changed from one of seeing me as an annoyance to one of seeing me as an asset. The reason it changed was because he started understanding my point of view. As a customer, I had lots of business to bring to him, not just now, but over the years. And he could endanger that business by handling this one transaction in an inappropriate way.

Customers aren't just people who buy. They are assets. And the real job in building a business is building ongoing, profitable relationships with your customers. What's in it for you in building customer satisfaction?

1. You retain more customers.

2. You increase your awareness of the importance of your customers.

3. You learn how to protect your current customers from your competitors.

4. You increase your understanding of the role that service has in this sales process throughout your company.

5. You enhance your reputation as a caring, conscientious sales consultant.

6. You discover the best way to handle customer complaints.

7. You learn the many ways that follow up after the sale ensures customer satisfaction.

8. In focusing on customer satisfaction, you discover creative ways to improve service and therefore increase sales in your organization.

pH Balance: Profits High, People Happy

An ad that has run on TV for many years talks about the importance of a woman's deodorant being pH balanced. What this means, of course, is that it has the right ingredients that make it compatible with the chemistry of a person's body.

I believe a business should also be pH balanced, and for that matter, your selling should be pH balanced: pH = Profits High. And pH = People Happy.

pH Balance

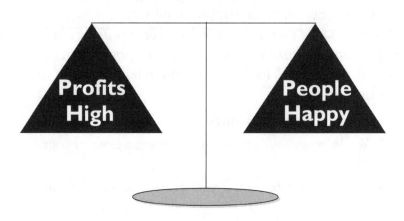

Certainly what you do should cause the profits to be high. But at the same time, it should cause the prospects who become your customers to be happy with their choice to do so.

In any given situation you need to balance those two. Many times when you just focus on the numbers, focus only on the profitability of each transaction, you can make the wrong decision, and actually lose a sales relationship with someone. At other times it's the best thing you can do. Sometimes you need to look at how many calls it takes to make a sale. You need to look at how many assets are in use when you are doing your selling; in other words, how many resources are you using up, how much time are you committing to each sales process? How many customers do you see in a typical day, or week, or month? When you look at the allocation of assets and the return on those allocations, the kind of profit you're getting, it tells you how to more efficiently use your time.

However, on the other side of this balance scale is pH, People Happy. And if all you're doing is trying to produce high profits, but the people aren't happy, pretty soon you're going to start losing sales and the profits will drop. So look at the People Happy side of the equation:

First, do your customers know that you care about them? If so, how do they know, what are you doing to show them that you care?

Second, do the customers truly feel understood by you? It's one thing to understand someone, it's quite another for them to *feel* that you understand them—that's where the real power is.

Next, look at the customers you're calling on and the way you're calling on them. Are you an enhancement to their day? When you show up, do you look like good news to them, or do you look like an interruption?

Also look at yourself. Are you happy with what you're doing? If you're not, alter the ways you're doing it. Find a new way to motivate yourself, find a new way to keep yourself focused on the customer, find new ways to add some joy to what you're doing day to day. If you don't feel very connected to what you're doing inside, chances are good it's showing up outside and others can tell you don't have your heart in it.

Learn to keep the people happy, both yourself, and the other people you're dealing with. Learn to keep the profits high. When you keep those two things in balance, business is beautiful.

What Is a Customer Worth to You?

Some years ago, I went into an automobile tire store. I needed some tires and I needed a number of other things for my car. As a matter of fact, I had a list of twenty-five items that my car needed. There were little things like a little switch here, or a little piece of paint was chipped over there, this thing wasn't running quite so well and that thing didn't look as good as it could look, and so forth. But the one thing that was at the top of my list was tires, I needed tires.

So I went to a tire store and found a set of tires at a reasonable price. Back in those days, the entire set of four tires cost only $239. I went in and talked to the guy who was going to install the tires. This was one of those buildings where they have three service bays where they put the car on a rack and they lift it up with a hydraulic lift to put the tires on easily.

I was standing outside the service bay, behind a little white stripe painted on the concrete in the safe area for customers to stand, and I was watching Mike put the tires on my car. Well, Mike got all the tires installed and did a nice professional job of it, and he turned around to me and said, "Excuse me, sir, is this your car? Would you come here a second?"

I stepped under the car and I was looking up at the underside of my car as he was pointing out some things to me. He said, "Next time you have it in for service and it's up on a rack, check this area to see if there's any wear, because it looks like there might be the beginning of some wear. You don't need to do anything now, but later on you might need to address that."

And I said, "OK, what do I need to do today?"

He said, "Like I said, nothing. You're fine, you've got your tires, everything's good, I just wanted to help you enjoy your car and keep it safe."

I was impressed.

I said, "By the way, I've got a list here of twenty-five items I need to get done to this car, could you refer me to someone to fix these other twenty-four?"

He looked at the list and he said, "Well, sir, we're a full service organization here, we can do almost all twenty-four of those."

So what started out as a $239 tire purchase, ended up on that same visit as a $1,600 renovation. And over the years, every time I needed service, I brought my car back to that particular dealer. I ended up spending $9,620.72 in parts and repairs on that car.

I know you might be thinking, it was a lemon. Well, I liked

the car, and the little repairs from time to time didn't annoy me that much. Plus the car was paid for, so the service was like car payments in some ways.

Nonetheless, I was worth $9,620.72 to that dealer. If they had simply installed the tires and sent me on my way and thought of me as a tire customer, I would have come back the next time I needed tires. But, I never had to buy tires again for that particular car. So I wouldn't have come back.

As it was, because they recognized that I was more than a tire customer, I was worth a great deal more to them and they could do a great deal more for me. They cultivated that initial relationship in a way that led to the rest of the relationship.

Carl Sewell, an automobile dealer extraordinaire, wrote a book called *Customers For Life*, in which he guesstimated that a typical automobile buyer spends somewhere in the neighborhood of $332,000 in their automobile-buying lifetime, just on automobiles.

Today that figure would be even larger. When you're talking about that kind of money, whether you're talking about cars, financial services, or independent business services, whatever it happens to be, does it really make sense for you to quibble with someone over details when there's a problem or disagreement? No.

It's best, whenever possible, to give in early, and provide them with the value that they need. Make sure you're making a reasonable financial decision in doing this, but serve your customers with the ultimate value of that customer in mind, not just the current value of today's transaction.

What is a customer worth to you? Take some time to think about what you could do for someone if they bought everything you could offer. And see just how much business potentially exists within your current client base, and your current marketplace. And then look for creative ways to expand that value.

Exceeding Customers' Expectations

Service is not a competitive edge, it is the competitive edge. People do not buy things, they buy expectations. One expectation is that the item they buy will produce the benefits the seller promised. Another is that if it doesn't, the seller will make good on the promise.

KARL ALBRECHT AND RON ZEMKE, *Service America: Doing Business in the New Economy*

If you think about what your product or service does for someone, the basic value someone gets from it grows out of the product or service itself. There are things that people expect from that; and if they don't get what they expect, then they're disappointed, and they lose a sense of connection with you or your company.

For example, if you're buying an automobile, you expect the automobile to perform without breakdown. You expect that it will function well, that it will perform in the way that cars are designed to perform. And it will look the way that it looked when you bought it, it will keep that look as long as you clean it and service it.

If it doesn't do that, you become dissatisfied. Now, if you buy an automobile, and not only does it do what you expect, but it also *exceeds* your expectations, then you can get really excited about it. You'll start telling your friends and neighbors about it, then you'll start building more sales for the company that sold it to you.

The same thing is true for services. If you buy a membership in an organization, and by being involved in that organization you get more than the expected benefits, you spread the word. But if you get less than the expected benefits, you also tend to spread the word.

The Technical Assistance Research Program out of Washington, D.C did one of the classic studies on this during the '80s. They found that the average satisfied customer would tell between five and twelve other people how happy they are with their product or service. But an average dissatisfied customer will tell somewhere between thirteen and twenty other people how dissatisfied they are.

When you look at dissatisfied customers, don't just think of one person being unhappy, think of one person starting to spread the poison of a bad reputation for you. So stop any of the bad news and start the good news in every way that you possibly can. And then ask yourself, what can I do that's a little bit extra? How could I, not up-sell them, but up-serve them and provide them with more benefits?

Assuring After-Sale Satisfaction

Let's look at following up and staying in touch after the sale.

Whether you're a salesperson or a front-line customer service representative, you need to understand some of the things that can go wrong after the sale. Customers become disgruntled for a number of reasons, most of which turn out to be minor, once they're handled tactfully. Your patience and understanding of human nature will help you remain calm when panic-stricken customers call and demand service.

"Selective perception" is a common mindset that customers adopt after a purchase. What this means is that they perceive one thing to be primary. A good way to practice this is, sometime when you're at a large sporting event sitting in the stands, look at the stands across from you, and as you're looking at all those people displayed there, think of one color at a time. Think white, and look for only the color white in the stands. It will jump out at you. And then think red, and then think blue, and then think black, and then think yellow. As you think about the different colors and you pause to look for them, you will see that color stand out in your consciousness. This is called "selective perception": you perceive the one color, you selected it and you focused on it.

> ## CASE STUDY
>
> ### CFX, Inc.
>
> One company that has seen impressive results from proactive communication is CFX Inc., a Miami-based importer of fresh-cut flowers from Central and South America. CFX holds training sessions for the top fifteen percent of its wholesale customers on all of the intricacies of the flowers they sell. "People don't realize that there are two hundred varieties of roses on the market in any given day," says Barbara Montes, CFX's sales and marketing manager. "New products are becoming available faster than anyone in our channels of distribution can learn about."
>
> The sessions, which are usually held at the wholesalers' sites, have yielded anywhere from twenty-five percent to one hundred percent increases in sales to participating wholesalers. "These are dramatic increases when you realize that our overall sales increases have been running five to ten percent for the past five years," Montes says. "As our industry grows, we've seen that it's important to work most closely with our highly committed customers."
>
> Source: "CFX, Inc. / USA Floral Products Brief," *Thompson Financial Investext,* June 6, 1998

Sometimes a customer could get a wonderful piece of equipment that does exactly what they want it to do, but they might have one little item that's annoying them about it, maybe the color's not quite a perfect match for the other things in their office. Maybe there's a noise it makes that somehow grates on their nerves. Maybe it takes a little bit too long to warm up for their personal preferences. Whatever it is, they tend to make that one item the all-important item upon which they focus and they forget about the other benefits that they're getting from the product or service. This "halo effect" tends to obscure the benefits of the product.

Since they expect their purchase to be perfect, the more they spend, the greater their expectations of perfection. As sales-

USAA

USAA, an organization in San Antonio, Texas, that provides financial services to U.S. military personnel and their families, keeps its database fresh by periodically surveying its three million customers worldwide. The company seeks updated information about customers, such as whether they have children (and, if so, how old they are); if customers have moved recently; when they plan to retire. USAA then tailors its marketing pieces to clients based on the surveys. If, for example, a family has college-age children, the association sends those children information on how to manage credit card debt.

"Some unnamed companies in financial services think it's appropriate to give credit cards to college students without teaching them to use them responsibly," says Phyllis Stahle, USAA's senior vice president of marketing. "When we issue credit cards, we spend a lot of time and effort explaining to students what their responsibilities are."

Similarly, USAA sends members booklets on things like financing a child's college education if those members have young children, or on estate planning if they're retired. "I know it sounds hyperbolic, but there's a sense of family with USAA," says Howard Gross, an attorney in Farmington, Connecticut, who's been a customer for roughly twenty-five years. "I get barraged by entreaties from various insurance companies, but USAA's mailers always seem to say, 'We're here to serve you.'"

Showing such care for customers is good business, Stahle says. She should know: USAA, a roughly $7 billion organization, retains 97 percent of its customers. "We build loyalty by convincing [customers] we're loyal to them," Stahle says.

Source: Dwight Gertz, "Strategic Growth," *Journal of Business Strategy*, (March/April 1997)

people, we need to put things in context for them. When someone lodges a complaint, check it out to see if it's a valid complaint and a correctable problem. If the customer's complaint is exaggerated, you may have to do some re-selling. Put the negative detail in perspective by pointing out the positives, the benefits.

You can also compare your product or service to your competitors, and show your customer how nothing would be gained by switching companies or suppliers.

In addition, you can suggest creative ways of solving the problem. Maybe you could move the offending noisemaker, or you could soundproof the area somehow.

Another common source of frustration for customers is user error. If you've ever bought a computer, you can easily relate to this one. Computer users usually go through hours of anxiety while they're learning to use the new system. This is why a formal training or orientation program should accompany installation in an office for everyone who will use it. You see, part of your job as a salesperson, when confirming sales of a technical product or service, is to try to avoid user error. So you must evaluate your customer's technical ability and recommend training or provide it if necessary.

You must also make your customer aware of the learning period required. For example, with a cell phone, or with using a new service, or with belonging to an organization—help them recognize what the rules and expectations are, help them recognize where they can find their answers, then they're much more able to solve their own problems.

This is equally important if your customer will be tracking results that prove or disprove your claims of performance. The true test of your product or service will come only after everyone is using it correctly. That's part of your responsibility as the salesperson.

There's another phrase you often hear—*buyer's remorse*. It's a catch-all phrase; it encompasses all the reasons why a customer might regret having made a purchase.

It doesn't matter if the reason is selective perception, user error, or simply the fear of having made the wrong decision—if the buyer feels it, you've got a problem to solve, and it's your responsibility.

"People respect sincerity, Hopkins, and, hey, I really mean that."

The bottom line is that the customer has not yet realized the benefits of the purchase, so it's your job to assure them that you've provided the solution, and the benefits will become apparent soon enough.

The more specific you can be the better, and this is a perfect time to remind your customer of your service guarantee or to show your customer once again the good reasons that they chose to do business with you.

Warning Signs of Dissatisfaction

Here are some warning signs to watch for, which might indicate that your customer is becoming dissatisfied:

Decrease in purchase volume. Because external factors may affect your industry, decreased sales may not be a reflection of dissatisfaction with your product, but you're never going to know that unless you check it out. So if external factors are not the reason, you may have a situation in which a complaint has gone unresolved or some other concern exists.

Increase in complaints. This is obvious, if the number or frequency of complaints increases, you have to quickly and effectively resolve the situation.

And, go one step further, if there's an operational flaw in your company, or in your product, work to have it corrected. Chances are good that more than one customer is having the same problem. How many are quietly taking their business elsewhere?

Repeated comments about the merits of the competition. Whether you hear it directly from a customer, or through the grapevine, this is a sure sign that somebody is getting ready to defect. If the competition's grass looks greener, you have to get out there and resell your company. Increase the perceived value, build trust again, bend over backwards if the account is worth it.

Decline in the business relationship. If you find that your customer is a little less cordial during your sales calls, or less receptive on the phone, find out why. Either you're making a pest of yourself or you're not in touch with them often enough, or they've become less enamored of your product, or they're looking at some other alternative. Find out why.

New management. This happens to all of us. It may not be a sign of dissatisfaction, but when new management comes into your customer's company, you need to pay close attention. Your task may be as simple as introducing yourself with a phone call or letter, or assuring them that their satisfaction is your highest priority, or you might be required to start from scratch with this new manager. Build trust, identify needs, understand their needs, solve them, gain a commitment, and sell them all over again.

Change in ownership. Whenever your customer's company is sold or absorbed by a larger firm, you need to establish a new working relationship with the new people. Sometimes the same people are still there, but the reporting responsibilities have changed.

Companies often start over by soliciting bids for the products or services that they have, and many times that puts you at risk. So maybe they're not a new prospect, they're an existing company, but you've still got to do your homework as if they were a brand new prospect.

One advantage, however, is that your product or service was already in place before the change, which is a selling point that you ought to be able to use, assuming your track record was good.

Keep your eyes and ears open and watch for warning signs of dissatisfaction before it becomes a firm statement of dissatisfaction.

Fifteen Ways to Stay Close to Customers

Here are fifteen ways to stay close to your customers.

1. *Show them that you think about them*—send a fax, an e-mail, a helpful newspaper clipping, tasteful cartoon, Christmas card, Thanksgiving card, birthday card. Send a card on the anniversary date of the day they became your customer.

2. *Drop by to show them what's new*, always make an appointment or call first, but do it when you're going to be in their neighborhood. Show them a new product or leave a brochure, or show them how to get another benefit out of what they already have.

3. *Follow up a sale with a free gift to enhance the purchase.* Customers often do not use their purchases correctly.

4. *Offer valued-customer discounts*—coupons, letters, sales promotions, something that would stimulate them to place additional orders or do more business with you.

5. *Let customers know they should contact you when they hire employees,* so then you can train their new people for free in how to use your product or service, you can give them an

Ward Howell International

Ward Howell International, a New York-based executive recruiting firm, grows its revenues by becoming virtually enmeshed with its customers. While most executive recruiters place people in corner offices, collect commissions, and then move on, Ward Howell actually helps its customers reorganize their entire companies.

For instance, the recruiter started placing executives at Harley David-son Inc. (several) years ago. When the relationship began, the quality of Harley's motorcycles had deteriorated; the bikes were (considered) inferior to Honda's, the market leader at the time.

So, executives from Ward Howell visited (all) of Harley's major plants and interviewed workers and engineers. They also spoke with dealers and members of riding clubs. Their conclusion? The problem wasn't with the rank-and-file workers, but with the company's leadership.

"We sat down with senior executives and said we'd build a team that would make a first-rate brand and superior product," says David Witte, Ward Howell's chairman and CEO. "We recommended that Harley find new people for officer-level positions in areas such as manufacturing, sales and marketing, and product design. When we suggested the personnel changes, the executives said their list was the same as ours. So we went out and got them some super people, like a top product design guy from Corvette."

Not long after, Harley became the market leader. In the past (several) years, it has broken the $1 billion revenue mark and doubled in size. While Witte is loath to take credit for his client's success, he does say, "We sit in with senior managers when they do their quarterly operational reviews, and find out what leadership competencies they need. We're their arms, legs, eyes, and ears. We go out and find the very best talent to meet their needs."

Rich Teerlink, Harley's (then) chairman, president, and CEO, (had) no problem giving his recruiters access to the company. "They've performed well for us," he says. "At the start of the relationship, they took the time and made the effort to learn about us, and they've earned our trust."

Ward Howell (invested) considerable resources in Harley, too, devoting an 18-person team of executives and researchers to the account. Witte himself works closely with the company's board of directors.

The recruiter's devotion has paid off. In seven years, it (had) placed 38 executives at the motorcycle maker—and none of them has left. "This is a long-term relationship, not a transactional sale," Witte says. "We're a consultant to Harley."

Source: "New Stratergy Announced at Ward Howell," *Business Wire*, May 5, 1998

orientation or provide them a briefing, or communicate with them by phone to help them understand the value that the others are getting.

6. *Compensate your customers whenever they lose time or money.* If they lost time or money from problems with your product or service, have a recovery program built for your customers and stick to it. Err on the side of generosity rather than losing your account.

7. *Be personal.* Keep notes in your customer file on everything from spouses' names to hobbies, to schools they went to, personality differences, and so forth.

8. *Always be honest.* Nothing undermines your credibility more than dishonesty. Lies always come back to haunt you at the worst possible moment.

9. *Accept returns unconditionally*—the few dollars you may lose in the short run are far less than what you could gain from acquiring a new customer.

10. *Honor your customer's privacy*—if you've been told something confidential, keep it confidential.

11. *Keep your promises*—baby sit deliveries and promised services if you have to, see that they get done, your reputation is on the line.

12. *Give feedback whenever you get referrals*—show your appreciation, tell the customer what happened, when they referred you to someone. It's also a good way to get more referrals.

13. *Make your customers famous*—well for fifteen minutes maybe. If your company has a newsletter, ask your customer for permission to write about their success with your product or service in the newsletter. Then send copies of this to your customer. The same can be done for industry publications.

14. *Arrange periodic performance reviews.* Meet annually, at least, with your customers to review how they're doing.

15. *Keep the lines of communication open.* Assure your customers that you are open to all their calls about anything and everything: ideas, grievances, advice, praise, questions, and so on.

"Clients can be a little prickly
at these Account Review sessions."

Maintain that all-important rapport. Remember, people do business with people they like.

Annual Account Reviews

I believe it's really valuable to conduct an annual review of and with each of your customers. Once or twice a year, evaluate your accounts to determine their A-B-C status—which ones are paying off the most for you, and which ones the least.

And then, once or twice a year, you should also meet with your customers, at least your best customers, to review where things stand. This gives you a chance to evaluate the account activity, the industry in general, the economic climate, get a sense of what to anticipate, competitor strengths and weaknesses, and so on. This is identical to the research you did when they were still prospects for you, but now you meet with your customers to get their input as well. You're collaborating in this review.

This meeting is an opportunity to keep the relationship strong, to ask for feedback, to get new ideas for new products or services, to give them new ideas about products, services, or features that they could add, and to shape the direction of future business with them.

You can also use this as a great time to gain referrals and testimonials. Every review meeting is different, but take the general guidelines that follow, and use these as often as you can.

If possible, arrange the meeting to be over breakfast or lunch. Eating tends to relax people and it gives it a more informal tone. Select a place that's conducive to the meeting, whether it's a meal or not. It should be well lit, with a large table, and a place that won't rush you out after your meal.

Invite all the significant participants from your account. If there are two buyers, make sure both can attend the meeting.

Bring all the spreadsheets or documents that are necessary to discuss your previous year's business. In addition, bring documentation to substantiate any claims that you may be making regarding trends or product reports or other things that you want them to consider.

Allow an adequate amount of time for the meeting. An hour might be rushing it; then again, an hour might be plenty.

Organize your presentation—this is not just a casual visit, it's an important business event. Use your time logically. Ask questions about how you've been performing, how your product or service has served your customer: the level of quality, how they are satisfied. Ask about their business and their future, what's new, what plans, what players, what changes.

Give them plenty of time to talk. Ask open-ended questions that draw your customers out and encourage them to say whatever is on their mind. Take notes or record the meeting, after getting permission.

Send a copy of the notes to your customer as a follow-up, summarizing the points.

Convey through your actions and your words that you are committed to serving the customer and you want a long, beneficial relationship with them.

After the annual review, introduce a new product, service, or marketing idea. But do not make this primarily a sales call. Make it primarily a relationship-strengthening call.

You can also offer them, as a sort of a payment for their co-operation in this review, some kind of a special discount or a promotional package, something to say thank you.

Look for opportunities and needs that go beyond the obvious ones. Focus on the big picture of what you're trying to do for your client and what they're trying to achieve for themselves, as well as looking at small details.

And when appropriate, ask for referrals or testimonial letters. Ask them if they mind if you document and publish the success they had with your product or service, so you can share that with others. Your present customer base is one of the best resources for new business for you.

Make sure that you review with each one of them how you're doing, and how you can get better.

Resolving Customer Problems

You know every person encounters customer problems. These are problems that a customer has had with your product or service or problems that a customer is having interpersonally with you or one of the people in your company. Whether or not you follow the right steps in resolving these problems determines whether you will keep that customer's business or lose it.

Handle the person first, then the problem. If a person is angry or upset, let them vent for awhile. This alone will go a long way toward resolving the problem. Problems seem a lot less severe after your customer has had a chance to tell you how they feel.

Next, *apologize*. This part's often left out, but it's a crucial gesture. It's not just enough to say, "I'm sorry this happened." Offering a sincere, personal apology, not just one on behalf of the company, is all that is needed to show that you are committed to the relationship.

Third, show *empathy*. Assure your customer that he or she has every right to be angry, or disturbed, or disappointed, and you would feel the same way if it had happened to you.

Fourth, *find a solution*. Resolve the problem *with* your customer, not just *for* her. Ask questions that will get her involved in the process. For example, "How would you like to see this problem resolved? What would be an acceptable resolution to you? If you were in my position, how might you resolve this kind of problem for your customer? Would a refund be acceptable to you? How can I compensate for this problem to help you be happy once again with our product?"

Jump through hoops, if necessary, take over and make the recovery process easy for your customer. If there are phone calls to make, forms to fill out, you assume the responsibility, you do the work. If the resolution of the problem is going to be complicated, explain the system to your customer so they understand how it is complex.

Stay in touch. People feel much better when they're informed than when they're kept in the dark. Imagine sitting on an airplane out on an active runway waiting for your turn to take off. But you're a passenger, you're not a pilot, there's a delay and yet another delay, and you're not informed. How would you feel? Well, at first you would trust in the pilot. After a while, you'd become concerned. A little later still, you'd ring your call button and you'd talk with the flight attendant and ask, "What's going on?" If you didn't get a good answer, then you'd start becoming upset. And ultimately, at some point you'd be venting your frustration or at least hoping to.

If you keep people informed as to what's happening, and how it's being handled, their frustration is often diminished.

Offer compensation. If what happened was bad enough, call personally and say, "I'm sorry" with some concrete gesture like offering a discount or giving a gift or going out of your way to provide an extra service to make it right. And it should be immediate; giving a gift long after the fact loses the meaning and makes it appear insincere. If you're going to give a gift, give it immediately after the problem. Make it meaningful—a meaningful gift is something that has a high, personal, perceived value to your customer. It doesn't have to cost a lot of money, but it should be meaningful and valuable to the customer.

It should also differentiate you from your competition. Be creative, customize the gift. Don't just send flowers or a box of candy, a lot of people do that. Know your customer well enough to determine whether a pair of tickets to a baseball game or a hot air balloon ride would be an even better gift.

The gift should be consumable. If you send a calendar or a clock to say I'm sorry, every time your customer looks at the calendar, for an entire year, they will be reminded of the problem they had with you. Save those kinds of gifts for different occasions, positive occasions. When you give a customer a gift to say I'm sorry, make it something they can consume, something to eat, or something that will be used up soon.

It should also be inexpensive. The combination of a high, personal value to them and a low cost to the company is ideal. Giving away more of your company's products or services may be appropriate and inexpensive, but do it only if they won't cause further problems. The worst thing you can do is offer your customers more of something that has already caused them grief.

And finally, *follow up.* After resolving a problem, with or without a gift, follow up personally. Make sure things are OK, and look for additional needs that represent future selling opportunities. Follow-up is essential because there's nothing worse than a fouled-up recovery. A recovery mess-up is guaranteed to lose you a customer.

The happy news in all of this is that when a customer has a problem, the problem becomes resolved and the customer feels good about the resolution, that customer feels more of a sense of allegiance and loyalty to you and your customer than the customer who had no problem whatsoever.

So look upon problems as an opportunity to strengthen your bond with the customer.

Handling Problems by Phone

Here's a way to handle customer problems when dealing with customers on the phone. You may or may not answer your own phone. If someone else does, that person should be trained to give customers the best impression.

If you answer the phone, you need to take time to do it properly. There are no excuses for rude or unprofessional behavior. Either use common courtesy or don't pick up the phone at all.

The five basic impressions a caller should receive from you are:

1. I will not waste your time.
2. I care about your and your business.
3. I am competent and well organized.
4. I can be trusted to help you get through to your party or solve your problem.
5. I'm proud of my company and I enjoy working here.

There are some "shoulds" that almost everyone needs to know when it comes to the phone.

Answer phone calls in no more than four rings. If your phone traffic is too heavy to allow this, hire someone else or get some way developed to get the call answered before the fourth ring. A good receptionist is not measured by how quickly he or she handles calls, but by the positive outcome of each call.

The same thing is true with salespeople. Be prepared, you look silly when you have to search for a pen and a notepad. Keep them near your phone. Similarly, if prices or other information are commonly requested over the phone, keep that information handy. If you're often answering calls on a cell phone, keep that information handy so you can quickly refer to it in the field.

When you answer the phone, identify yourself, or your company, or both. The caller should know immediately who took the call. It gives information but also adds a friendly, personal touch. Screen calls tactfully, if you're going to screen them. It's better to make a request or ask a question than to sound demanding. Instead of, "What's this about?" you might say, "Will the person you're trying to reach know what this call is in reference to?" By the same token, "May I tell him who's calling," is more polite than, "Who's calling?" Anything can be said nicely if you try.

Don't make customers repeat their stories. One of the most frustrating things for a customer occurs when they call in and talk with one person, tell their whole story, and then are transferred. You get referred to another and you have to repeat the entire story. If you're referring a call up the line to someone else, when you refer the call, tell the person you're referring it to what you've already been told. When they answer, they can say to the customer, "Hi, Mr. Customer, I understand that you're having a problem with the first part of the installation process, let me see if I can help you."

Maximum hold time, fifteen seconds. Yep, fifteen seconds. If you have to put somebody on hold, put them on hold very briefly. Otherwise, ask them for their number and call them back. Better yet, ask for permission to call them back. You can say, "I'm right in the middle of something right now that I can't interrupt, may I take your number and get right back to you?" Give them a courteous response, show them you respect their problem and their needs, and that you'll get back to them right away. And then, for heaven sakes, do it. Time spent on hold is often referred to as being in "voice jail," and that's what it feels like when you're waiting endlessly to get your message through.

Also, when you answer the phone, or when the other person answers the phone, get in the habit of asking, "Is now a convenient time for you to talk about this?" Or if they're calling you, "May I ask a few questions to determine how we can best explore the roots of this problem?"

Train, test, and coach. Train yourself, test yourself, have other people call you and observe your calls. Then coach yourself and get coaching from other people who are good at telephone skills. Train others well, tell them exactly what you expect, don't assume that people know how to answer the phone well, test them by having a friend call to see how they're treated on the phone, and have others do the same thing for you.

Using these insights to train yourself and coach other people will vastly improve your telephone skills.

When to Fire a Customer

When should you fire a customer? Interesting thought. Fire a customer!? In reality, some people are really not good potential customers for you. When a customer is too demanding, rude and abusive, many times it makes better sense to refer them to someone else or to politely decline doing business with them and happily move on to another more productive contact.

If someone is continually critical, abusive and unpleasant, you need to reevaluate. Do you need their business desperately enough to put up with that, or is there no justification for continuing that dialogue?

Usually, the bigger the discount they want, the bigger the aggravation the account will be once you get it. It's common practice to deeply discount prices sometimes in order to gain a prospect's business. But, too often, the resulting aggravation will be in direct proportion to the size of the discount. It's as if some customers devalue your goods and services if you discount deeply.

Many people expect even more allowances for future business. Remember, you can choose not to do business with an account if the payoff doesn't outweigh the expenditure or the time investment in it. By the way, be sure your employer approves of this decision before acting on it.

Be careful not to discount just for the sake of discounting, or to simply use it as an excuse for not being a good salesperson. *If you keep dropping the price on anything far enough, sooner or later most everybody will buy. That's not selling, that's simply finding out the lowest level of price at which they would automatically buy, where a salesperson would be unnecessary.*

Focus on selling solutions and value. Get your price. It's there for a reason—you deserve it.

Does the client do business the way your company does business? If honesty, integrity, and candor are important to you, as they should be, and your client suggests cheating his company or your company or a third party—you're headed for major problems down the road. Don't do business with people like that.

When it comes to bad customers, actually I'm talking about people who probably shouldn't have been your customer in the first place. I think you should apply *Cathcart's First Rule of Commerce: Never, ever pay people to make your life unpleasant.*

Think about that, when you spend time with someone. You're paying them for whatever you get from them. When you spend resources on someone, you are in effect paying them for whatever you get in response. When you put your time and energy into serving a customer, you are in fact "paying" them for whatever they pay you in return. If you're getting nothing but unpleasantness back, maybe this person shouldn't be on your customer list.

A few years ago I was in the office and Susie, who worked for me, came in, and said, "Jim, there's a man on the phone who demanded, 'I want to talk to Jim!'"

I asked her, "What's it about?"

She said, "He called, and he said, 'let me speak to Jim'—that was his opening. And I said, like you have always asked me to, 'Certainly, may I tell him who's calling?' He roared, 'Just put him on the phone!' and I said, 'One moment.'"

Upon hearing of his rude behavior, I told Susie to stand right there and let me handle this call in her presence.

I picked up the phone, and said, "Hi, this is Jim."

The man on the other end said, "Hey Jim, how's it going?" He then started a false friendliness kind of a sales spiel.

I said right back, "Excuse me, did you just say to my colleague, Susie, 'Just put him on the phone!'?"

He said, "Well, I deal with a lot of high-powered executives who don't want their subordinates knowing their personal business."

I said, "Well, I find that really insulting and I would appreciate it if you would never call here again, because in this place of business, we respect our coworkers." And I hung up.

Susie looked at me, smiling from ear to ear.

I said to her, "Susie, the next time somebody calls and behaves like a jerk, you have my permission to say to them, 'Sir or Madam, I have the authority to terminate this telephone call, would you like to approach this a little bit differently?'"

When people are truly unpleasant toward us, if the unpleasantness is really out of line, not just a dissatisfied customer who's voicing a complaint, but someone who's being downright rude and obnoxious, I believe we should eliminate those people from our customer or prospect list. Some of them are just not worth the energy that it takes to get their business.

Sometimes we have to tolerate a few of those little outbursts, just to keep the customer well served and to keep them happy.

"I think I've found a way to resolve our personality differences."

There are moments where everybody has a bad day or a bad mood. But, when it truly gets out of line, I think we need to draw the line. If we don't respect ourselves, and our own coworkers, they have no reason to respect us either.

These are only a few of many possibilities open to you. You need to know where are your boundaries, what are the standards by which you operate, what are the types of behaviors that a customer might do that would cause you to say, "I think you'd be happy doing business with someone else instead of us."

Sometimes it does make sense to let a customer go to someone else. When the cost of keeping them requires you to compromise your principles, or involves a great deal of grief on your part, maybe it's a good idea to pass this one up and go on to the next sale.

The irony is that many times, when confronted with the awareness that they have been obnoxious, customers will change their behavior. People want to be liked, but sometimes they charge boldly ahead with no awareness of how they are affecting others. In times like those, they need a wakeup call to get them back on track.

■ ■ ■

THE EIGHTH COMPETENCY

Manage
Lead, Motivate, and
Grow Yourself

Improve Yourself for Selling

LET'S TALK ABOUT YOU AS YOUR OWN SALES MANAGER and your degree of effectiveness in managing yourself as a salesperson. This is personal and professional development. Here are some of the key areas you need to manage:

1. Maintaining a positive mental attitude, keeping yourself in a good frame of mind.

2. Keeping your customers in a positive frame of mind. Managing their point of view, their perspective on you, your product, and your service.

3. Your current level of professional credibility, as viewed by most of your prospects or customers. How good are you at building and sustaining professional credibility?

4. Your relative ability and mastery in selling. As a salesperson overall, how effective are you in doing all the various parts

that make selling successful? What's your relative ability and mastery in motivating yourself as a salesperson? Can you get yourself to do what needs to be done, even when you don't feel like doing it? Can you get yourself up early and out into the marketplace in a regular, consistent way?

5. How good are you at managing yourself as a salesperson, keeping track of the numbers, knowing what's working, knowing what's not working?

6. What's your overall awareness and understanding of your company's philosophy, its mission, its strategies and the primary values that drive your company? The better you understand the thinking and the concepts behind your company, the better you'll understand the operation of your company.

7. How well aware are you of the internal structure and operations of your company? How does it function? Do you understand who does what and how things get done internally? The better you understand its internal workings, the more effectively you can work within it.

8. How good are you at developing a personal marketing plan, a comprehensive plan for getting yourself to the sales level you want, the professional credibility you want, the professional equity you need to attain to achieve your own personal goals?

9. Self-education. How well do you keep yourself learning and growing? They say if you're not growing, you're starting to die. Growth is the natural unfolding of life, and it's important that we intentionally participate in our own growth. So how well do you keep yourself learning and growing?

10. Self-motivation. How effective are you in keeping yourself motivated to do what's needed, when it's needed, in the way that it's needed? How well do you keep yourself upbeat and positive, keep yourself constantly going forward and exerting new energy to do the things that you need to be doing?

Think about yourself as a salesperson and then ask: How effective and competent am I right now, in being my own sales manager? As you evaluate yourself in each of these ten areas, consider which require you to sharpen your skills today to be a more effective salesperson tomorrow.

Self-Leadership

The ability to get yourself to do what needs to be done, when it needs to be done, whether you feel like it or not, and still do it well.

Selling by the Numbers

It's amazing how many times success can be assured by attending to the basics.

A study a few years ago of 257 Fortune 500 companies found that seventeen percent of salespeople do not predetermine the approximate length for each sales call, the duration. Twenty-three percent of them don't use a computer to assist in time and territory management (of course, that number changes every day as technology expands). Twenty-eight percent do not set profit goals for their accounts. Thirty-seven percent do not use prescribed routing patterns in covering their territories. Forty-six percent don't look at their use of time in an organized fashion. Forty-nine percent, almost half, do not determine the economical number of calls for each account, they just keep calling until they make a sale or they give up too early. Forty-nine percent do not use prepared sales presentations—did you get that?—forty-nine percent do not use prepared sales presentations. They're winging it! Seventy percent don't schedule their calls very effectively. Seventy-five percent don't have a system for classifying their customers according to the sales potential of each customer—seventy-five percent! Seventy-six percent don't set sales objectives for each of their accounts. And eighty-one percent don't use a call reporting system. So how are these people managing themselves? The answer, I believe, is ineffectively.

Measurement helps you determine what you're doing right and what you're not. If you don't keep records, you don't have a clue as to how to improve.

There are many methods to measure and evaluate your performance. Sometimes your customer relationship management software or sales force automation software can do it for you. Sometimes just a simple database manager can give you much information; it tells you exactly what you need to do to get better. But so many people use only a small portion of what's available to them, whether it's through their computer, on the worldwide web, on a handheld palm computer, or in a written text where they keep documented paper evidence of what they do. The method you choose should complement the ones used by your company or your sales manager.

The five areas for any manager to measure are sales calls, expenses incurred, non-sales activities, new market opportunities, and the results you're getting. To interpret your records, look for two things: How has it changed from last year? What ratios do you have currently? Your ratios may be the following:

- Calls to contacts
- Contacts to presentations
- Presentations to times when you ask for the sale
- Times you ask for the sale versus the times that they say yes
- Times that they say yes versus the amount of your average profit on each new account
- Each new account versus the number of new accounts that stay on the books a year later

"Hard figures are not available, but Henry's poem explores the essence of our situation."

When you look at these ratios, a bad ratio between one and the other tells you what to work on to be a better salesperson.

A low sales-per-appointment ratio may indicate, for instance, that you need to improve your presentation skills. If the number of calls you're making per day is low, you're simply not picking up the phone or opening the doors often enough; you need to increase the number of calls. Any result will improve if you increase the number of calls you're making, the number of efforts going in. Sales can be a numbers game, keeping records will show you how these numbers apply to you.

Why Goals Matter

Generally speaking, people don't give much thought to what they really want. That's why so much emphasis is put on goal setting in the business community, especially in sales. If you don't know what you want for your life, your career, if you don't know

213

what you want for this particular sales contact, chances are good you will not be very focused on achieving it. So give some thought at this time to what you want from your life.

What do you want? Do you want lots of professional involvement. Do you want recognition from certain groups of people, or acceptance by certain individuals? Do you want to be included in a certain group? Do you want to achieve specific things, milestones, accomplishments? Do you want to win certain awards, or do you want to attain a certain level of financial success?

What do you want in your life, what kind of relationships, what kind of lifestyle, what kind of key events? What matters to you is at the core of these questions. What matters? When you think about what matters to you today, and you actually take the time to write it down and date it, it helps you organize everything else you do.

There's a concept known as Chaos Theory, which holds that though things happen at random, there is often a pattern within the chaos, which can be understood and used as we prepare for an "uncertain" future.

We know when we go out to make a sales call that it's highly unlikely we're going to be attacked by Huns. It's highly unlikely that we're going to be caught in a volcanic eruption. But we do know what we will encounter. *We know that we will encounter people who are afraid to make a financial commitment. We will encounter people who are overly impressed with our competitor's products. We know that we will encounter people who dislike talking with salespeople because they're afraid they'll be manipulated into a sale,* and so forth.

The same principle that makes a sales career predictable in that way applies to goal setting. When you set a goal, you give a commonality to all the behaviors in your life, you give a reason to the processes, and you give a why to the how.

If every day you're getting up, going through the same general motions, eating your morning meal, going about your business, doing generally what you do every day and ending the day in a similar way, the pattern stays the same unless there's a reason to change it. *When you give yourself a bigger goal, a more compelling reason to do something differently, the behaviors will start to organize themselves around the new reason.*

If you have a child born into your family, all of a sudden lots of things in your life change because now you have a new reason to do things—the welfare of that child. My wife and I recently were informed of the arrival of our first grandchild and that has stimulated a series of wonderful changes in our world—some inconvenient, some convenient, but all of them very meaningful. Once he was born, we found ourselves looking for a new home closer to where he and his parents live. Yet we hadn't even considered moving from La Jolla during the preceding nineteen years. (We moved in less than four months!)

Goal setting is at the center of meaningful living. If there is no goal, there is no reason. With a goal, you have a "why" behind the "how." Everything gains meaning and sparkle.

It really matters that we take all this complex philosophy and simplify it in the one way that all human beings can—by setting specific goals. What do you want in your life? What do you want to happen? What do you want to achieve? What do you want to experience? What do you want to have? What do you want to see? What do you want to do? And more than that, what do you want to be?

Take some time now, and every year spend some time setting goals. You don't have to worry about working out whether you can achieve them or not. If it's something you want, write it down. It organizes all the chaos. It gives meaning to the message. It gives you a reason for doing what you do each day to improve your life.

*First say to yourself what you would be; and then do
what you have to do.*

EPICTETUS

Your Daily "Thought Diet"

*The thought manifests as the word.
The word manifests as the deed.
Deed forms into habit.
And habit hardens into character.
So, watch your thoughts with care.*

THOMAS MERTON

When a person wants to change their body shape, or change their nutrition, they go on a diet. So when a person wants to change their achievement level, I suggest they go on a *thought diet*. It has nothing to do with your food, but has everything to do with your thoughts.

The thought diet is a simple process by which you can organize your thinking and focus your actions to get the outcomes that you want.

The first step in the thought diet is that you write things in terms of what you want, not what you want to avoid. For example, you state your goals in the positive: "I will breathe only clean air today," would be much better than saying, "I will not inhale smoke today."

They must be stated in the present tense. "I swim a half mile a day and love it." If that's your goal, to swim a half mile a day, don't say, "I will," say "I do." Every time you read it, it reaffirms your belief in the possibility of doing it.

In your thought diet, your affirmations, like any goals, should be specific, measurable, and personal to you. "I call five new prospects every day" would be an appropriate statement.

"All I want is the chance to prove that money can't make me happy."

When you develop your thought diet, the first thing to do is get a little card upon which you can write on both sides. On the top of side one, write your current primary goal. What is the one thing you want most in your life at this current time? Write the goal as if it had already happened, put today's date on the card so you know when you wrote the goal, then move to the bottom half of side one.

On the bottom half of side one, identify five qualities or traits that you would have if you had already achieved that goal. Write these traits down as goals for you to achieve—in other words, if one of those traits is keeping a positive attitude, write it down. If one of those traits is getting up early in the morning and getting a quick start on the day, write it down. If one of those traits is being respectful to other people, write it down. But still, identify the five traits that are most likely to make you eligible for achieving the goal at the top of that page.

Then flip the card over to side two. On side two, identify the eight areas of your life—mental, physical, family, social, spiritual, career, financial, and emotional. Think of one thing you could do in each of those areas of your life today. Something that would be easy to do, something that would be productive to do, but would not require a great deal to motivate yourself to get it done.

Write down some simple, minimum, daily activity in each area of your life and then get yourself every day to do those minimum activities. If you find after a few days that you're not doing those minimum items, lower the standards for now. Make it easier to do. The key to this is to get yourself started on the diet, to start doing something to feed your mind, start doing something to exercise your body or nourish it, start doing something to nurture your spirit, etc., so that every day you're working a little bit on all eight areas of your life.

Some, of course, will get a lot more attention some days than others do. That's natural. But every day, pay a little bit of attention to each area. As you do each of these minimum items, you will acquire each of the five traits listed on the other side of the card, and developing those five traits will make you more eligible to achieve the goal that you're seeking to achieve.

The diet works very well if you have a continuous flow from the goal to the role, the traits, then to the activities. Keep this card in your pocket at all times. Look at it morning and night, and keep yourself thinking, every single day, for one month, about exactly what you need to be doing to grow in all eight areas, to acquire those five key traits to achieve the goal that matters most to you right now.

The Thought Diet™ Card

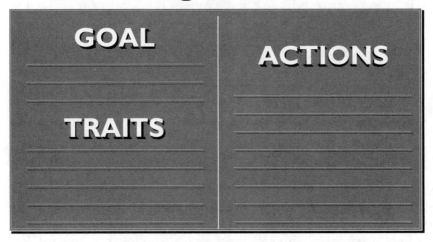

GOAL

ACTIONS

TRAITS

The Thought Diet™

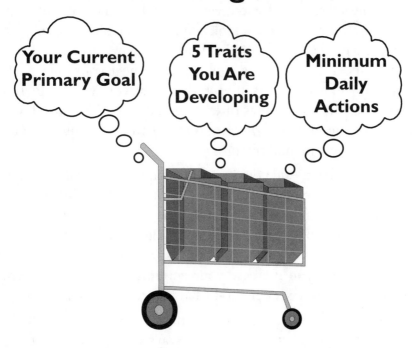

Your Current Primary Goal

5 Traits You Are Developing

Minimum Daily Actions

How Success Is Made

Changing yourself doesn't just happen. It is a result that must be made—M-A-D-E.

M—*mental pictures*

A—*affirmations*

D—*daily successes*

E—*environmental influences*

Developing sales leadership is not something that happens to you, it's something you make happen. Like any type of change, it's not necessarily easy; but change is a fact of life, something we must all learn to welcome and implement more readily. The key is to control the change rather than waiting for it to control you. By staying in control, you make change an ally, rather than an adversary. Here are the four items once again:

M—mental pictures. First, create a new mental picture of yourself. Visualize how you will look and feel in the outcome that you desire. If you desire to be a sales leader, visualize how you'll conduct yourself on sales calls, how you will meet your sales goals, how you will carry yourself each day, what you will do. Picture yourself as the new you as often as you can. Make a storyboard of images, pictures, and descriptions that will help you see yourself in this new mental picture.

A—affirmations. Add your new self-image to your daily thought diet. When you talk about yourself to others, do so in a positive way, without bragging or boasting, just talk in positive terms. Don't hesitate to discuss the changes you're making to advance your life. By making your goals public so other people know what your goals are, you increase your commitment to fulfill them. Affirm what you're seeking, not what you're trying to avoid.

D—daily successes. Success comes in small increments. So build confidence every day by setting up ways to experience success.

That means practicing sales mastery behaviors every day. *Use the many ideas that you get from* Relationship Selling *and be sure to reward yourself for your successes.* Treat yourself to a pleasurable experience from time to time and keep yourself doing some little something or some major something every day of your life to build a habit of succeeding.

E—environmental influences. Make your environment help you succeed. Surround yourself with positive influences. Avoid people and situations that make you uncomfortable or make you feel a lack of self-esteem. Find support in people or groups who influence you to believe in yourself more and to think more positively about achieving your outcome. Surround yourself with positive statements, inspiring sounds (like listening to audio messages and inspiring music), pictures that conjure up images that give you a positive expectation. The more these influences are in your environment, the more likely they are to help you succeed.

If you have the clear mental pictures; if you affirm through the way you talk the outcomes that you want instead of the outcomes you fear; if daily you're practicing the success habits and surrounding yourself with environmental influences, you will in fact find that your success has been made—self-made. *They say every person is self-made, but as Earl Nightingale says, "Only the successful will admit it."*

Roles, Responsibilities, and Expectations

Every sales relationship needs to be consciously designed and managed. When we take conscious responsibility for building our relationships, we can create the types of connections that we want. We can manage our existing relationships so that they grow to be healthy and productive. The clearer your understanding of your role in the relationship, the better the relationship will be.

Let me describe to you a concept that I call *role descriptions*. This concept can be used by managers, salespeople, you and me as individuals to define what we do, how we do it, and why we do it.

Three categories need to be defined to design a successful new sales relationship. First, define your role. Second, identify your areas of responsibility. Finally, clarify the expectations that you and the other person have from this relationship. The more clearly you define these three categories, the better you will manage your relationships and further their growth.

Number one: Define Your Role

What is it you do? Who do you do it for? How do they benefit from that? Although many salespeople define their role as "making sales," the professional salesperson defines his or her role as "building a profitable clientele." There's a big difference between just making sales and building a profitable clientele. It involves establishing ongoing business relationships that are profitable both to the company and to the customer.

Number two: Define Your Areas of Responsibility

Practically every aspect of your organization's operations could fall within the description of building a profitable clientele, because that's generally what businesses or organizations do. But to do this, you need to specifically define *your* areas of responsibility. This might include identifying and contacting prospects, assessing their needs, generating sales, assuring delivery or installation or orientation, whatever happens after the sale, following through to guarantee that the customer is satisfied, and so forth.

Number three: Clarify Expectations

On a blank sheet of paper, write down expectations that are likely to arise in the relationship—on your part and on the customer's part. On one side, list what you expect from your company and from your customers. On the other side, list what your customers and your company can reasonably expect from you. Look for discrepancies in the two sets of expectations and discuss them with your manager, your supervisor, a colleague, or a friend.

Repeat this exercise often to clarify expectations that are likely to arise in a relationship between you and a customer.

Self-Empowerment—The Eight T's

When it comes to motivating yourself, here are eight words (each starting with "T") that you can use for self-empowerment. *Any time you want to empower and motivate yourself for more achievement, simply ask these eight questions to determine what aspect of empowerment would have the most value for you.*

T—Target. Are you clear on the target, the goal that you're trying to achieve? If not, make sure you've focused your attention on the specific outcome you desire.

T—Tools. Do you have the tools or information needed to do your job well? Do you have what you need to be ready to perform at a high level?

T—Training. Have you received enough training or orientation to be able to use these tools and information very well?

T—Time. Have you had enough time for the training to take effect, for it to sink in, for you to try and succeed, try and fail, try and adjust and succeed again? Without the proper amount of time, success is not likely.

T—Truth. Do you know the truth about how all of this really fits together? What happens when you're finished with your part? What happens before you get involved in the project? What is the truth about how everything fits together and works?

T—Tracking. Are you getting the feedback that you need in order to stay on the beam, to be on-project, on-goal? Are you measuring and getting the feedback that tells you when you're on track and when you're off?

T—Touch. The human touch. Are you getting the support and encouragement you need? Are there other people you're in touch with who can help you achieve your goal?

And *T—Trust.* Do you trust yourself appropriately for your skill and mastery level? Do the others around you trust you enough to give you the kind of resources you need?

The Marketing, Sales, and Service Mix

Marketing, selling, and service are not the same thing. *Marketing* is generating a desire for your product or service. *Selling* is converting that desire into transactions. And *service* converts those transactions into satisfied clients.

There are five ways to mix sales, service, and marketing, but only one of those five will guarantee you success.

If you have great marketing, but poor sales, that equals poverty. You don't even get to do the service because great marketing, generating demand, won't pay your bills. If you're not converting demand into sales, you're not going to have much success, and there'll be nobody to serve.

Great sales, with poor marketing, equals burnout. Marketing can help you open doors by creating demand; but without marketing, everything is on your shoulders. Selling never gets any easier for you because nobody's helping. It depends solely on your daily activity.

Great marketing plus great selling, followed by poor service, equals surprises. Unpleasant surprises at that. A dissatisfied client will come back to haunt you every time. This usually happens when you least expect it, when you're least prepared for it, and when it's most embarrassing to you.

Great service with poor marketing and poor sales equals loneliness. If you're tremendous at doing what you do for clients, but there's not good marketing to set up the demand, and there's not good selling to actually turn that into customers, then you're in trouble. That's what I call the "Maytag Syndrome." Remember those ads, the Maytag repairman who's sitting there alone, nobody's calling? The reason he's sitting alone is because the products are so good they never need service.

Here's the final one: Great marketing plus great selling plus great service equals success. The dynamic mix of marketing to generate the demand, selling to convert that into purchases, and service to assure that the customers are satisfied and stay satisfied, that's what it takes to generate outstanding results—that will make you successful.

Managing Yourself: Be Your Own Sales Manager

Be your own sales manager. You may have someone you report to who fills the role of sales manager in your world, but it's also important that you become your own sales manager. *As a sales professional you have two major responsibilities. One, to get yourself to make sales. And two, to develop yourself as a salesperson, so you're worth more each day you are in business.*

As you grow in your knowledge of selling, you have to grow in your ability to manage yourself as a sales performer. These are separate jobs but permanently intertwined. The less effective you are in managing yourself, the more dependent you are on others to keep you at the top of your form.

The less effective you are in selling, the more energy you will waste, the more calls you will make unproductively, and the far too few the sales you'll produce.

Keep these two in balance throughout your sales career: making sales and managing yourself as a salesperson. Think of yourself as the owner of your own company, under contract with your current employer. And then ask, "How can I constantly increase my value to the marketplace?"

Keep a log of what you do with your time. As your own sales manager, look at what you're doing as a salesperson. What do you do first thing in the morning? What do you do when you first get to work? How do you learn every day? How do you build learning into a typical day? What do you do during your first call? How effective is your first call compared to your fifth or tenth call? What do you do with your lunch hour? Is it used productively or non-productively? How many breaks to you take? What do you do during your breaks? How do you organize your materials? How do you control the scheduling and routing of your activity so that you're using your time efficiently and you're going about your business in an efficient manner? How do you maintain the tools and equipment with which you sell? How do you keep yourself in shape as a salesperson? How do you maintain the right appearance, the right attitude, the right tone of voice?

Once you've made a log of what you do every day and how you use your time, it's very helpful to look back at the end of each day and reflect, **first**, on what went right today, and why? Celebrate those successes, get clear on what you did right.

Second, ask, what went wrong today, and why? Identify where you're messing up. Reduce the likelihood of that happening again.

Third, ask, at what time today did I start working on my top priority task? How come so late? Could I have started earlier?

Fourth, what patterns do I see in my time logs as I look at how I use my time day after day after day? What do I see as a regular pattern that keeps occurring all the time?

Fifth, what part of my day was most productive? What part was least productive? Is it the same approximate time every day?

Sixth, what were my three biggest time wasters today?

Seventh, which activities of mine need more time? Which ones could do with less time?

And **eighth**, beginning tomorrow, what will I do to make better use of my time?

Once you've identified your most productive and least productive activities, it's pretty easy to manage yourself into more productivity.

How to Win a Sales Contest

Every sales contest shares identifiable phases. It usually starts with a bang, slows down in the middle, and winds up with a big push.

Winning a sales contest is easier when you understand what to emphasize in each phase. Now there's no question that sales contests motivate people. But they have a dark side as well.

All too often, a sales professional puts so much energy into the contest that they burn out and suffer a big slump after the contest ends. Many people find that they're most productive during the annual contest and relatively unproductive the rest of the year. Not good.

True professionals know how to maximize the contest and beat their own previous performance. They also know how to use a contest to crank themselves up to a higher level of overall sales achievement, not just during the contest.

To emulate these true professionals, check to see when your next sales contest is scheduled. If none is planned, hold your own sales contest. Pick a period when you're usually a little less productive, identify a time frame and challenge yourself to pull out all the stops and see just how good you're capable of being. Use these phases to plan your activities for each part of the sales contest:

First, prepare. Before the contest begins, inventory the skills, the knowledge, and the tools and information you will need to be at your absolute best throughout the entire contest.

Second, build an inventory of qualified prospects. People who lose sales contests typically do so because most of their prospecting is done in the early part of the contest. Instead of making sales, they're still trying to figure out to whom they could be selling. Those who win do this before the contest. Identify all the prospecting methods you can use to build an inventory of qualified prospects—before your sales contest begins. Spend several weeks identifying potential buyers, contacting them to determine whether they're qualified, preparing them to receive a sales call from you during the contest period. Often prospecting alone is enough to generate new sales that otherwise wouldn't have come about. So do your prospecting.

Third, clear your calendar. Take a look at the obligations that are occupying your time and which ones contribute to future sales. Which ones could you delegate to someone else or postpone to a later time? By eliminating inhibitors, you can free yourself to focus only on selling.

Fourth, focus on the kickoff. Start the contest with a sales blitz by making lots of calls in a short time. Free your entire schedule so that the only thing you do in the opening days or the first week of the sales contest is think, talk, walk, and breathe selling. When you plan your schedule, fill the entire day with quality sales contacts. When you get up in the morning, meet a prospect for breakfast. When you work out, do it somewhere where you can talk with a prospect. Have lunch with prospects, spend the afternoon with prospects, have an early dinner with prospects and relax that evening and regroup for the next day. Gain agreement from your family to focus all your energy on selling during the contest's first week. Get them involved in the process, have them help you develop lists and gather information. Have them help you make phone calls and confirm appointments if appropriate. Urge them to help you identify more prospects and prepare for the next day's selling. Treat this as if you were an athlete going into a major championship. Put all your focus on being able to be your best.

Five, avoid mid-contest slump. During a long contest, over several weeks, there's always a point where the initial energy wears off, things grow less exciting, and a sales slump looms. Be careful, prevent this slump by planning enough activity into each day to ensure a constant flow of new contacts, follow-up calls, and other activities. Keep yourself on the selling track.

Six, make the final push. At the end, concentrate on writing up business, confirming sales, following through to make sure that the business is truly confirmed. As you did in the opening days of the contest, free your time to focus on selling. Now is the crunch, this is the final push, find helpers who can do the detail work and follow up for you so that you can spend your time helping customers make the buying commitment. If several steps are involved in completing a sale, put together a short-term team to help accomplish those steps. Be sure you eat well and get plenty of sleep each night so that you're at the top of your form each day.

Seven, build customer satisfaction through delivery and follow-up. As you celebrate and rest at the end of the contest, be sure to follow through on every purchase. You want everyone who bought during the contest to be happy about their purchase and satisfied with its value.

Eight, after it's over and you have a chance to reflect, evaluate your performance. What worked and what didn't? Use the lessons you learned about keeping yourself at a higher level of productivity, the lessons you learned about being your best, and apply those year round. Change some of your regular habits and routines, keep yourself at these higher levels of sales productivity. That's how the true professionals grow and that's why they beat their previous performance in every sales contest.

Think Net, Not Gross

Years ago I had a sales representative working for me. He was an excellent seller, but he tended to get really excited about the gross sales volume, rather than the net profit on sales. He'd say to me, "I made a sale today of this much money!"

And I would say, "Will we get to keep all that money?"

"Well no, this much has to go to the speaker's bureau that booked us, and this much has to go for product costs, and that much has to go for distribution, and this much for commissions, but I made a sale of THIS much money today!"

And I'd say, "Yes, but isn't the net about one-eighth the size of the gross in that case?"

I continued, *"It's great to get excited about the sale, but let your excitement be about the reality of what was made, not about the amount that just shows up in the gross revenue category."*

Once, I was doing a series of speaking engagements around the country, and in each city when I stopped, I got a little something and sent it to him by mail. The first thing I sent him was a hair net, just a simple little hair net, no note, just a little inscription saying it was from me. About a week later I went to a pet shop and bought a scoop net for an aquarium, and I sent that to him. Next, I went into a sporting goods store and I got a fisherman's net and I sent that to him. A few weeks later I sent him an extremely disgusting picture, a "gross" picture, with a Post-it® note attached, saying, "This is gross."

After he received each item, he asked, "Why did you send this to me?" I would just say to him, "Think about it and we'll talk about it in a few days when I get home."

After I sent him the last item, and was back home, I walked into his office, and he said to me, "OK, end the mystery. What is this? What's the purpose of all these nets and things you've been sending me?"

"What I wanted you to do is start identifying the difference between gross and net. I wanted you to stop thinking only about gross dollars on each sale, and start thinking about the net profit."

Profit is the key to effective selling, and for you to be more effective and earn a higher income, you need to be more motivated by the net profit, not just the gross revenue.

Are you aware of the net revenue you produce when you make a sale? Or do you tend to focus on the gross? The more you understand about profitability, the better you can use your time, target your energies, and increase your own sales commissions.

Get a sheet of paper and indicate the gross amount generated by your typical sale. Then note next to it the net profit generated by that sale. Discuss these figures with your sales manager or coworker, and see if you can determine all the costs that are incurred, all the things that you have to do with your time, with your money, with your resources, in order to generate that sale and service it appropriately. See what real net profit is left after all costs have been paid. It will give you a much clearer picture of where the money is and how to generate a lot more of it.

Lead with Your Heart, Guide with Your Head

Several years ago I was walking on the beach in La Jolla, California with a colleague of mine, Dr. Spencer Johnson, who wrote the book *Who Moved My Cheese?* and prior to that, many other books, including co-authoring *The One Minute Manager* with Dr. Ken Blanchard.

We sat down in front of the La Jolla Beach and Tennis Club and watched the sunset. And he said to me, "I've been studying people who do what you do."

I said, "You mean professional speakers?"

He said, "Yes, trainers, speakers. Most of them seem to be working really, really hard but not getting as much in return for their effort as they could get. Then there's a small group of them who seem to be getting almost everything they want, seemingly without effort."

I asked, "Why do you think that is?"

"What I've found is that the large group, the people working hard and getting minimal results, seem to be working primarily in their head. To them, it's all about logic, systems, linear thinking, details, specific hard plans and doing exact behaviors in an exact way. That's useful, but that's not what gets big successes in the long run."

"What about the smaller group that seems to be getting everything they want and not working nearly as hard to get it?" I asked.

He said, "Jim, those people seem to be coming primarily from their heart. They're doing the things they love to do and they're doing things in a way that they deeply care about and feel committed to."

The same principle holds true with *your* customer. People love to buy. They love it because buying is fun. It gives them a feeling of satisfaction. They buy to gain that satisfaction rather than simply to satisfy a logical need. Most of the time, it's not their head that's doing the buying, it's their heart. Their head is analyzing the decision, but their heart is making the commitment. It's an emotional commitment rather than a logical one, much of the time.

Buyers use logic to analyze, examine, and research the buying decision, so that when their heart says it's time to go ahead, they feel safe in doing so. The best way to deal with this is to lead with the heart but guide with the head throughout the sales process. Use emotional appeals to help your buyer decide to make the purchase. Appeal to their wants and their needs, show them that you care about them and what they get, that you're doing something good for them.

Then when your buyer steps back to examine the purchase, appeal to their logic. Show them how your purchase enhances their life, presents possible problems. Give them documentation, proof, testimonials, warranties, whatever you can. In your presentation give them the logical foundation to make the emotional commitment to say yes.

In your next sales presentation, remind yourself to first talk about "why." Those are the issues of the heart. And then focus on "how." That's the domain of the head. Your logic won't persuade the buyer, but it will help your buyer persuade him- or herself. It's the emotion that causes the person to say "yes" today.

Lead with your Heart
Guide with your Head

Begin Another Growth Cycle

Once you have gone through a process as comprehensive as the one outlined in this book, you are forever changed. Old attitudes have gone away, new skills have emerged, a new way of looking at your career and yourself has emerged. That means you are ready for another growth cycle.

You have graduated; this is your commencement, not your retirement. So now is a great time to start the growth process anew. Take time to reflect on what you have covered as you applied these ideas. Tag or highlight the specific ideas or exercises that you would benefit from doing again. Consciously resist the temptation to set this book down forever. Many of its exercises will serve you year after year. And make sure, especially, that you apply what you have learned.

The best way to do this is to "Kick the L Out of Learning." *Lifelong learning is essential in today's world, but there must also be some lifelong "earning."* One of the jokes on many college campuses is those people who become "professional students." They seem to be going to school as a career, or actually, in place of one. These individuals make the assumption that if they will just learn enough, the money will come. Year after year, they enroll in yet another series of courses or advanced programs without ever taking on a full-time job.

Now don't get me wrong, lifelong learning is the only way to assure that you don't become obsolete. The "students" I'm talking about are the ones who never seem to graduate or go to work, not even as a full-time educator. *When there is no graduation, there is no commencement of one's career.*

These noncontributors have their counterparts in selling. They are the salespersons who assume that, if they will just learn enough about their product, industry or sales skills, abundant sales will follow.

This is both wrong and dangerous thinking. Simply put, *sales don't come from what you know; they come from what you do. Knowing makes you more capable but action brings results.*

I say, instead, let's kick the L out of learning. The difference between learning and earning is that one pesky letter, the L. If we could just learn to remove it at the appropriate moment, then our income would increase.

The next time you consider a class, or pick up a book, or listen to a recording, or even chat with a colleague, ask yourself, "What am I going to DO with this knowledge?" Think in terms of application, not just concepts. Start holding your own feet to the fire, so to speak. Make yourself accountable for taking action on what you know.

Without action, knowledge leads to intellectual arrogance. It brings out the critic in you and separates you from others and from reality. Have you ever noticed that critics are most often pessimistic and skeptical, rather than supportive and optimistic?

The critic counters by saying, "I'm not a pessimist. I'm a realist."

Do you know what *a "realist"* in this sense really is? *He is a pessimist who won't admit it. Somehow the "realists" never take the positive point of view.*

Their lack of participation, involvement, or commitment to the activity causes them to be "Monday morning quarterbacks." They say, "You should have made a pass yesterday instead of trying to run the ball on that key play." And you might reply, "You may be right. Now that I've had twenty-four hours to think about the decision and I'm no longer in the heat and pressure of the game, I would come to the same conclusion. But it's too late now, isn't it?" It's easy to criticize.

The solution is to get into the game . . . and stay there.

When you find yourself doing more learning than earning, stop and ask yourself, "How am I going to USE what I have learned . . . right now?" Keep yourself action-oriented and, as you continue to learn, occasionally kick the L out of learning.

"How would the person I'd like to be . . .

. . . do the things I'm about to do . . ."

Jim Cathcart

Cathcart Institute • 800-222-4883 • info@cathcart.com • www.cathcart.com

■ ■ ■

The Author: Jim Cathcart

High achievers from around the world credit the advice and inspiration of Jim Cathcart as keys to their personal advancement. As the author of thirteen books on business and psychology, including two best sellers, *The Acorn Principle* and *Relationship Selling*, Jim Cathcart's works are in use by businesses and universities worldwide.

CEO and founder of Cathcart Institute, Inc., Mr. Cathcart sits on several corporate boards plus the Advisory Board of the University of Akron, College of Business, Fisher Institute for Professional Selling.

He is one of the world's top professional speakers and business authors and has been inducted into the Speaker Hall of Fame, received the Golden Gavel Award from Toastmasters International, and the Cavett Award from the National Speakers Association. Mr. Cathcart became a member of Speakers Roundtable, twenty of the top professional speakers in the world, in 1986.

Cathcart Institute, Inc., founded in 1977, is a network of highly qualified business advisors who teach Jim Cathcart's concepts and strategies for Relationship Selling and personal advancement. The Relationship Selling Sales Excellence System is built upon the principles of personal accountability and structured to utilize all of an organization's learning resources, not just the material in this book. Business leaders and top salespeople turn to Cathcart Institute, Inc. for training, inspiration, and personal advice in their quest to reach the top one percent of their field.

With over 2,500 speeches delivered to more than 1,500 different clients worldwide, Jim Cathcart has reached hundreds of thousands of business professionals live and in person.

Among the companies founded and co-owned by Jim Cathcart are: The Professional Speaking Institute, based in North Carolina, and MentorU, a builder of private online learning centers, based in San Diego, California.

For further information, contact:

Cathcart Institute, Inc.
Speakers Office
6120 Paseo Del Norte
Suite B-1
Carlsbad, CA 92009

Toll free: 800-222-4883
E-mail: info@cathcart.com
Websites: www.cathcart.com
www.relationshipselling.com
www.professionalspeaker.com

Bibliography and Recommended Reading

Alessandra, Anthony; Baron, Gregg; & Cathcart, Jim. *The Sales Professional's Idea-A-Day Guide*. Chicago, IL: Dartnell, 1996.

Alessandra, Anthony; Cathcart, Jim; & Monoky, John. *Be Your Own Sales Manager*. New York: Fireside, 1990.

Alessandra, Anthony; Cathcart, Jim; & Wexler, Phillip. *Selling By Objectives*. Englewood Cliffs, NJ: Prentice Hall, 1988.

Alessandra, Anthony & O'Connor, Michael J. *The Platinum Rule*. New York: Warner Books, 1996.

Armstrong, Thomas. *7 Kinds of Smart: Identifying and Developing Your Many Intelligences*. New York: Plume, 1993.

Armstrong, Thomas. *Multiple Intelligences in the Classroom*. Alexandria, VA: Association for Supervision and Curriculum Development, 1994.

Brooks, Bill, *High Impact Selling*. Greensboro, NC: Game Plan Press, 1995.

Canfield, Jack & Hansen, Mark Victor. *The Aladdin Factor*. New York: Berkley Books, 1995.

Canfield, Jack & Miller, Jacqueline. *Heart At Work*. New York: McGraw-Hill, 1996.

Carnegie, Dale. *How to Win Friends and Influence People*. New York: Simon and Schuster, 1952.

Cathcart, Jim; Brooks, Bill; & Antion, Tom, *The Professional Speaker Business System*, Professional Speaking Institute, 1996–2002. *www.professionalspeaker.com*

Cathcart, Jim, *The Acorn Principle*. New York: St. Martin's Press, 1998.

239

Cathcart, Jim. *Relationship Selling*. New York: Perigee Books, 1990.

Clifton, Donald O. & Nelson, Paula. *Soar With Your Strengths*. New York: Delacorte Press, 1992.

Covey, Stephen R. *The 7 Habits of Highly Effective People*. New York: Fireside Book, 1989.

Csikszentmihalyi, Mihaly. *Flow*. New York: Harper and Row, 1990.

Dunn, David. *Try Giving Yourself Away*. Englewood Cliffs, NJ: Prentice-Hall, 1956.

Dychtwald, Ken. *Age Wave*. New York: Bantam Books, 1990.

Frankl, Viktor E. *Man's Search For Meaning*. New York: Washington Square Press/Pocket Books, 1985.

Gardner, Howard. *Frames of Mind: The Theory of Multiple Intelligences*. New York: Basic Books, 1983.

Horton, Robert. The InnerView Profile, Carefree, AZ, Carefree Institute, 1990.

Johnson, Spencer. *Yes or No*. New York: HarperCollins, 1992.

Jung, Carl *Psychological Types*. Princeton, NJ: Princeton University Press, 1971.

Kriegel, Robert & Kriegel, Marilyn Harris. *The C Zone*. New York: Fawcett Columbine, 1984.

Lee, Blaine. *The Power Principle*. New York: Simon and Schuster, 1997.

Lewis, Hunter. *A Question of Values: Six Ways We Make the Personal Choices That Shape Our Lives*. New York: HarperCollins, 1990.

Marston, William Moulton. *Emotions of Normal People*. New York: Harcourt, Brace & Company, 1928.

Merton, Thomas. *The Way of Chuang-Tzu*. New York: New Directions, 1969.

Newton, James. *Uncommon Friends*. New York: Harcourt Brace Jovanovich, 1987.

Nightingale, Earl. *Lead the Field* (audio series). Chicago, IL: Nightingale-Conant Corp., 1972.

Oakley, Ed. *Enlightened Leadership*. New York, NY: Simon & Schuster, Inc., 1991.

Pirsig, Robert M. *Zen and the Art of Motorcycle Maintenance*. New York: Bantam Books, 1974.

Rose, Colin & Gall, Louise. *Accelerate Your Learning*. Carlsbad, CA: Accelerated Learning Systems, 1992.

Senge, Peter. *The Fifth Discipline*. New York: Doubleday, 1990.

Sinetar, Marsha. *Do What You Love, The Money Will Follow*. New York: Dell Publishing, 1987.

Sommer, Robert B. (Ed.). *The Winning Spirit*. Glendale, CA: Griffin Publishing, 1996.

Speakers Roundtable. *Speaking Secrets of the Masters*. Harrisburg, PA: Executive Books, 1995.

Sternberg, Robert J. *The Triarchic Mind: A New Theory of Human Intelligence*. New York: Viking, 1988.

Stock, Gregory. *The Book of Questions*. New York: Workman Publishing.

Truax, Pamela Larson & Myron, Monique Reece. *Market Smarter Not Harder*. Dubuque, Iowa: Kendall/Hunt Publishing Company, 1996.

Vance, Mike & Deacon, Diane. *Think Out of the Box*. Franklin Lakes, NJ: Career Press, 1995.

Waitley, Denis. *The Psychology of Winning* (sound recording). Chicago, IL: Nightingale Conant Corp., 1983.

Waitley, Denis. *Seeds of Greatness: Ten Best Kept Secrets of Total Success*. Old Tapan, NJ: Revell, 1983.

Wattles, Wallace. *How to be a Genius*. South Windsor, CT: Inspiration House Publishers, 1955.

Weinberg, George. *Self Creation*. New York: Avon Books, 1978.

Wheatley, Margaret J. *Leadership and the New Science: Learning About Organization from an Orderly Universe*. San Francisco, CA: Berrett-Koehler Publishers, 1992.

Winninger, Thomas. *Hiring Smart*. Rocklin, CA: Prima Publishing, 1997.

More Ways to Learn Relationship Selling

The ideas in this book can be combined with individual exercises and worksheets to become:

Training-On-Call: a voice-mail call-in knowledge base, for phone or Palm Access,

E-Learning for Sales: a weekly e-mail series of audios or articles (enough ideas for up to 4 years),

Training-on-Tap: a series of skill sessions built into your self-management software for Laptop Learning,

A Web-based Skills Series for universal access 24/7,

Curbside Coaching program with Sales Readiness Assessment to identify areas of focus,

Self-improvement series,

A traditional training course,

A custom designed book or audio series for your own organization,

An audio series on CD or Cassette, or,

When combined with video footage of Jim Cathcart or a live presentation, a multi-dimensional mixed media training program.

For further information on Relationship Selling or Jim Cathcart contact:

Cathcart Institute, Inc.
800-222-4883
www.cathcart.com
www.relationshipselling.com
Email: info@cathcart.com

INDEX

market profile, steps in, 53–56
markets
  chosen market, 52, 53
  definition of, 51
  natural market, 52–53
mathematical/logical intelligence, elements of, 133
Maytag syndrome, 225
meetings, of sales team, 8
Merton, Thomas, 216
moderate velocity types, 126–127
Montes, Barbara, 188
motivation
  self–empowerment, 223–224
  self–motivation, 210
Motley, Arthur "Red, ," 20
musical intelligence, elements of, 133

N
natural market, 52–53
natural values, 129–132
  aesthetics, 130
  commitment, 131
  empathy, 130
  knowledge, 131
  power, 130–131
  sensuality, 129–130
  wealth, 130
need gap, in sales presentation, 145
needs assessment, 99–138
  customer needs, types of, 103
  goal of, 13
  and listening, 99–102, 110–113
  and monetary issues, 115
  questioning, tips for, 108–110
  questions to ask customer, 107
  topics to explore, 114–115
Negotiating Your Success (Hennig), 168
negotiation of sale, 168–171
  power factors in, 168–170
net versus gross, and sales, 229–231
nonverbal communication, buying signals, 167–168
note–taking, 110

O
objections to sale. *See* resistance to sale
openness, in communication, 117–118
operational bandwidth, 135–137
organic era, selling in, 26–27

P
pace of individuals. *See* personal velocity
perception power, 170
performance measures, 211–213
  areas to measure, 212
persistence, value of, 150
personality traits
  bandwidth, human, 135–138
  behavioral styles, 119–125
  and intelligence, 132–135
  natural values, 129–132
  personal velocity, 125–128
personal space, awareness of, 111
personal velocity, 125–128
  energy and drive in, 125–126
  high velocity types, 126
  low velocity types, 127
  moderate velocity types, 126–127
  seller–buyer match, 128
persuasion, partner versus persuader concept, 82–85
Peters, Tom, 106
pH balance concept, 181–182
Phelps, William Lyon, 94
physical intelligence, elements of, 133
Platinum Rule, 117–120, 129
Platinum Rule, The (Alessandra), 63, 117
power
  alternative power, 168–169
  commitment power, 169
  deadline power, 170
  expert power, 169
  knowledge power, 169
  legitimacy power, 169
  perception power, 170
  as personal value, 130–131
  relationship power, 170–171
  reward or punishment power, 169
  risk power, 169
preparation for selling, 33–49
  daily question, 42–45
  goal of, 12–13, 14
  preparation for excelling, 35–37
  and product knowledge, 45–50
  and professional equity, 37–40
  reputation, others' perception of, 40–41
  sales planning guide, 47–48
  self–assessment, 17, 36–37
  steps in, 33–35

Index